MISTRESS GINGER *Cooks!*

EVERYDAY VEGAN FOOD FOR EVERYONE

by Mistress Ginger

To Evelyn!
♡ Mistress Ginger
xoxo

Book Publishing Company
SUMMERTOWN, TENNESSEE

Library of Congress Cataloging-in-Publication Data

Mistress Ginger.
  Mistress Ginger cooks! : everyday vegan food for everyone / Mistress Ginger.
      pages   cm
  Includes index.
  ISBN 978-1-57067-302-3 (pbk.) — ISBN 978-1-57067-895-0 (e-book)
  1. Vegan cooking.   I. Title.
  TX837.M575 2014
  641.5'636—dc23

                                                           2013049291

Author photos: Erik Saulitis
Food photographer: Andrew Schmidt
Food styling: Ron Maxen
Cover and interior design: John Wincek

Pictured on back cover: Bubbly Bombshell, p. 55; Cha-Cha-Cha Chutney,
p. 126; Yam Wedgies, p. 70; Sloppy Gingers, p. 88; Tie-the-Knot Chocolate-
Peanut Butter Pie, p. 148

Book Publishing Company
P.O. Box 99
Summertown, TN 38483
888-260-8458
www.bookpubco.com

ISBN: 978-1-57067-302-3

Printed in the United States of America

19 18 17 16 15 14   9 8 7 6 5 4 3 2 1

Book Publishing Company is a member of
Green Press Initiative. We chose to print this
title on paper with 10% postconsumer
recycled content, processed without chlorine,
which saves the following natural resources:

   10 trees
   323 pounds of solid waste
   4,824 gallons of water
   889 pounds of greenhouse gases
   5 million BTU of energy

For more information on Green Press Initiative,
visit www.greenpressinitiative.org.

Environmental impact estimates were made
using the Environmental Defense Fund Paper
Calculator. For more information visit www.
papercalculator.org.

Printed on recycled paper.

CONTENTS

A Message *from Your Mistress*

Hello, darling peeps. It's me, Mistress Ginger. I'm thrilled that you are reading this book, touching the pages that I've so lovingly woven together with my own bare hands.

Be warned, this is not your typical culinary compilation. How could it be with me at the helm? I declare, I am not a chef! I'm just a traveling showgirl. But I do know my way around a kitchen. In fact, I've been using a vegan diet to fuel my singing and dancing for more than a dozen years, and I'm *still alive*! And not only am I alive, but I'm also thriving! I've got that vegan glow, as they say.

Who's "they," you ask? My lovers, of course! I can't tell you how many lovers discover that I'm vegan and immediately launch into some compulsory confession of their nutritional woes. They tell me how they are really carnivores, how they couldn't live without cheese, how they last ate a vegetable in 1994 and had such a massive gastrointestinal disturbance that they have gagged at the sight of anything green ever since. At the same time, they are drawn to my radiant vitality and want some of that for themselves. Invariably, they ask me to take them grocery shopping, explaining that they haven't a clue what to buy and wouldn't know what to do with a red bell pepper once they got it home. (This is all on the first date, mind you.)

In honor of these dear souls, I have penned these pages. Now, when these boys start their rambling, I just hand them this book. Herein, they find explicit instructions on how to proceed in the realm of vegan cookery. This book answers all their burning questions:

- What's this thing called vegan?
- What staples should I have in my pantry?
- What about all those freaky vegan specialty foods?
- What are some vegan recipes that I can make for myself any old day?
- Can I take you out on Friday night?

I imagine that many of you have similar questions (especially as to Friday night). Or perhaps you just think of this book as one of those hoity-toity art books that you can proudly display on your coffee table. I understand; the stunning photographs of yours truly sprinkled throughout are sure to create quite a stir at your next princess party. But guess what! This is an actual cookbook, and an actual *vegan* cookbook at that. Gracious, what have you gotten yourself into? Well, I'll tell you what you've gotten yourself into. *Mistress Ginger Cooks*, that's what! Now come along and cook with me!

Mistress Ginger Cooks is chock-full of practical advice for anyone who eats, which, I imagine, includes you. Now open your mind and your mouth to the plant-based paradise that awaits you. You're sure to find something that pleases your palate. What's more, you're likely to discover a thing or two about how you, even with all your day-to-day hustling and bustling, can incorporate more vegan food into your diet. Word to your mother!

In this book, I focus on simple, everyday dishes that the novice cook can make without much ado, and I've also included just a few elaborate recipes that you can toil over when you have a little extra time for something extra special, like when you need to wow a new lover. Pretty soon, he'll be asking *you* to take him grocery shopping. (And that's exactly why I recommend keeping a few extra copies of this book at your bedside.)

But take note! Eating well is not only a matter of preparing delicious, nutritious food. It also means eating a variety of well-balanced meals in portions and proportions that are right for you. Healthy meal planning for the busy vegan is one of my specialties. In this book I've not only supplied you with easy recipes that make for happy taste buds, but I've also included tips on meal planning, with practical suggestions for creating balanced meals each and every day of your snazzle-frazzle life.

I've written this book for everyone. Whether you're a longtime vegan who wears a crown of kale as a badge of honor or a self-described carnivore who doesn't know a radish from a rutabaga, may *Mistress Ginger Cooks* bring you titillation and inspiration, leading you to acquire that vegan glow for yourself. And if all else fails, you've got a smashing new conversation piece for your next princess party.

This Thing Called *Vegan*

The word "vegan." What does it mean? How could I define it? Well, if you want to talk about vegan defined, check out my abs, baby. Six-pack central. But seriously now, I'm talking about the word "vegan." What the hell does it mean?

First of all, how do you say it? It's pronounced *vee*-gun, not *vay*-gun, not *veej*-in, and certainly not *meat*-stick! Repeat after me: *vee*-gun . . . *vee*-gun. Very good. Now say it with joy!

Why? Whether or not you aspire to become a full-fledged vegan, you are in this moment connecting to something deep inside of you that compels you to read this book, to dabble in the realm of vegan cookery. Maybe you consider yourself altogether omnivorous but every now and then you like to whip up a batch of vegan cookies. You say, "Oh, I just made these delicious *vegan* cookies," and you say the word "vegan" as though Glinda the Good Witch herself, in her magic pink bubble, has just arisen from the depths of your consciousness and uttered the word "vegan" in a voice dripping with loving compassion. When I say the word "vegan," I'm connecting to that Glinda inside of me, to what I dream for myself and for this world.

Now who taught me what it means to live a life of compassion? My lovers, of course! I don't only date self-described carnivores. I've also had vegan lovers, and they told me about how there is suffering in this world. I had no idea! We can't escape it completely, but we can do our best to minimize the suffering that we inflict directly or indirectly.

Did you know that our food choices have a significant effect on the world around us? It's true. When we purchase meat and other animal-based products, we are in effect subsidizing an industry that treats animals like crap. The well-being of these magnificent creatures becomes secondary to the financial gain of the industry. It's the nature of the biz. These farmed animals are enslaved, exploited, and subjected to countless forms of abuse on a daily basis. No joke!

I will not delve into describing what transpires on factory farms. I want this book to be light and fluffy, like a sweet ride on a vegan cream puff. I do, however, recommend that you at least acquaint yourself with the reality of the situation. You may refer to the resources section (see "The Continuing Adventures of You," page 163) for a list of websites and publications that will further enlighten you about these matters. These very resources are what motivated me to go vegan. It was a natural response. I simply wanted to do whatever I could to help these animals.

Just think of it—little ol' me, Mistress Ginger, devastatingly beautiful show-girl, changing the world one bite at a time. Change happens in this way, with each and every step, starting with just one person, one glittering person. I am that person, and you are that person. If you don't believe me, take it from my favorite bumper sticker: "Dreams become reality one choice at a time."

Every trip to the grocery store is like stepping into a voting booth. When I opt for tofu over turkey, I'm casting my vote. When I choose chickpeas over chicken, I'm making a statement. When I say yes to almond milk and no to cow's milk, I'm having my say. Oh, the power! I love power, and I have the opportunity to exercise this delicious power at least three times a day, whenever I sit down for a meal.

I'd be remiss if I didn't mention that being vegan extends beyond dietary choices; it means refusing to support the exploitation of animals in every facet of life, and not just for the reason of animal cruelty. The well-being of our planet and our own human health are also compelling reasons to go vegan. In this book I focus on the dietary aspects of vegan living, but I invite you to learn more about all that the vegan lifestyle encompasses.

Now don't fret, my pet. This book isn't just for those who consider them-selves vegan or who are even on the road to becoming vegan. It's for anyone who'd like to do a little more good and a little less harm. We need not feel that our efforts have to be "all or nothing" to make a difference. If you can't do it all, just do *something*, dammit! Even one meatless meal a day is something—a very great something indeed.

That said, if you really want to go all the way, be my guest. It's funny how those words just roll off the tongue. But now when I say "go all the way," I'm speaking of veganism. And what would that mean, to go vegan all the way? In terms of diet, a vegan doesn't eat animals or anything that comes from an animal: no animal flesh, no dairy products, no eggs, no honey, and no animal by-products.

But now just think of all that you *can* eat. Gorgeous grains, beautiful beans, lovely legumes, fabulous fruits, vibrant vegetables, magnificent nuts, stupendous seeds, and anything else that comes from the plant kingdom. Food full of life! Eating a variety of these foods in portions that are right for our individual needs gives us the nutrients that will not only keep us alive but also help us to truly thrive in this world.

Now dig in and experience *your* inner Glinda!

Eat, drink, and be Mary

WHAT THE MISTRESS SAYS, *goes!*

I'm not a certified nutritionist, but I am certifiable. I mean, that's what I hear people say right after I meet them. They walk away saying, "Wow, she's certifiable!" I'm very proud of that, and I've started putting it on my résumé: Mistress Ginger, certifiable traveling showgirl.

For as long as I've been delighting the masses as a triple-threat diva, I've been delighting my lovers with hearty helpings of my vegan cookery. In that regard, I've finally reached the elusive quadruple-threat status: singer-dancer-actress and vegan know-it-all. With this credential under my faux snakeskin belt, I'm officially qualified to dazzle you with some dietary recommendations. Now please open your mind to receive the teachings that I'm about to hurl in your general direction. I'm going to bestow upon you Ginger's ABCs of balancing a meal, my approach to eating well for optimum health, vegan-style!

I'm also going to give you some advice on how to transform mealtimes, even if you're a busy bee like me. And oh boy, am I busy! I spend all day dancing and singing, and all night . . . teaching new lovers how to grocery shop. I don't have tons of time to toil over a hot stove, but I still manage to eat an all-vegan, mostly whole-foods diet. If this hot tot can make it work, so can you.

Words to the wise:

- Take it one step at a time.
- Set realistic goals for yourself.
- Don't try to be perfect; leave that to me.

3

Those of you who would like to try cooking more whole foods but are currently getting all your meals from the local gas station should expect to dally a tad more in the kitchen. Vegan or not, a diet consisting of mostly whole foods prepared at home is going to require more planning and time than grabbing a handful of grub at the nearby Pump-N-Munch.

Also, be aware that a dietary transition can be challenging. You may experience symptoms of detoxification as you adapt to more wholesome ways of eating. Avoid challenging yourself physically, emotionally, socially, or in other ways while undergoing this process of reinventing your diet. Ideally, you should adjust to this new way of eating before running a triathlon, birthing triplets, or dealing with Aunt Edna, who will be determined to stuff her honeyed ham down your throat anytime between Thanksgiving and New Year's Day.

In the beginning, you'll need a little extra energy for planning your menus, organizing your grocery lists, trying new recipes, and discovering how a vegan diet can work for you. Before long, your new habits will feel like second nature, and you'll hardly need to think about serving up good eats. Your body will find its way to balance, and you'll feel grand. You've spent who-knows-how-many years learning to eat the god-awful way that you currently do. Give yourself at least a couple of months to change up your habits and adapt to a new way of eating. There's no one plan that works for everyone, and everyone's individual needs will change over time. Consider the time spent exploring this new path as an investment that will yield priceless returns. Your body will thank you with energy and longevity, and you'll ultimately have more time to do all that you want to do.

Here they are, my ten tips for meal planning for the busy vegan:

1 **Enjoy yourself.** Calm your ass down and enjoy the ride! Have fun with this new venture. Let's throw shame, guilt, and perfectionism out the window. You're here! That's a great thing. Now explore with wonder all that this plant-based paradise has in store for you.

2 **Enjoy your leftovers.** Some people are averse to having leftovers. With great compassion, I say, "Get over it!" Wonderful meals can be made from leftover food, and you'll save time and money when you get strategic in this way. When you make a meal, prepare larger quantities so that you can easily pack a lunch or create a new dinner from what is left over. Understand that leftovers don't have to mean mealtime monotony. One part of a leftover dish can be transformed into an entirely different meal, and what a relief it is to know that you don't have to start from scratch.

3 **Have an easy breakfast.** Few of us have time in the morning to be cooking elaborate meals. Save the pancakes, scrambles, and hash browns for the rare morning that you do have that leisure time. On a typical day, when you're running around to shower, dress, check email, and feed the panda, a simple smoothie can be the perfect breakfast. I feel good when fresh fruit is the centerpiece of my morning meal, and with the Swoop-Me-Up Smoothie (page 25), you get just that. Throw the fruit in a blender along with a few satisfying sources of protein and fat, and you've got a power-packed meal that you can sip while you shave your armpits.

4 **Eat your greens, beans, and grains.** Let this be your mantra. At every lunch and dinner, try to get something from each of these three nutrient-dense food groups and then rest assured that you're getting a variety of essential nutrients in your diet. You needn't labor over elaborate dishes to make this happen. To see what I mean, take a gander at the Brazilian Rainbow Platter (page 100), a simple, beautiful, delicious meal that can be made in mere minutes! Listen to your Mistress: greens, beans, and grains. Follow this general guideline, and no one gets hurt.

5 **Fat is your friend.** Be good to your friend, and invite her to every meal. Fats help to make our food palatable and filling and give us good energy to burn. Whole-food sources of fat are always the best friends to have: avocado, coconut, olives, nuts, nut butters, seeds, and tahini, to name a few. Opt for these whole-food forms of fatty foods and minimize your consumption of refined oil, which is loaded with calories but otherwise has little nutritional value.

6 **Listen to your body, because every body is different.** These nutritional recommendations, even from someone as "certifiable" as me, are general guidelines that should be adapted in ways that feel right to you. Attune yourself to what your body needs, observing the effects of different foods on your energy levels, skin, hair, and immunity. When I'm dancing up a storm, doing multiple fan kicks and countless time steps, I need to eat more in general, and more calorie-dense food. Some days I crave more protein. Some days, more green veggies. Some days, more grains. I adjust the portions and proportions accordingly. I choose meals that reflect these cravings, and I ultimately feel good and look good, *damn* good!

7 **"Where do you get your protein?"** This old line seems to be everyone's favorite question for a vegan. If you should start eating more plants and fewer animals, be prepared to hear this question. Or maybe you're a newbie to vegetarian nutrition, and you yourself have this sincere concern. Heaven knows, I did! I wondered, how's a fierce showgirl like me going to get enough protein? I had been taught that I need to eat animals so that I don't waste away. Not true! Protein abounds in the plant kingdom. Beans, nuts, seeds, whole grains, and even many vegetables are sources of high-quality protein. By eating a variety of these foods while getting enough calories to meet your specific energy needs, you can get all the protein you need to be the exquisite specimen you were destined to be.

8 Eat both raw and cooked fruits and vegetables. While I want you to get cooking with Mistress Ginger, I also want you to get raw with Mistress Ginger. By that I mean that I want you to eat some raw food. (What did you think I meant?) Some fruits and vegetables offer more nutrition in the raw, while some nutrients are more easily accessed when cooked. Get some of each! I always eat raw fruit with breakfast and for snacks throughout the day. I also try to have at least one raw green salad a day. Of course, vegetables are also wonderful steamed, fried, grilled, baked, boiled, or roasted. Embrace variety and taste the rainbow. (You can apply this maxim both to eating and to dating.)

9 Bring a snack. The world is not yet fully vegan, and we need to be prepared for this reality when we're out and about living our snazzle-frazzle vegan lives. As you may know, I've played to every speakeasy and slaughterhouse this side of the Sahara (only the vegetable slaughterhouses, of course). Sometimes I find myself in places that have little in the way of vegan options, and I need to come prepared if I want to stay happily nourished. When I'm headed into unfamiliar territory, I make sure to bring snacks. By all means, come prepared and don't give anyone the impression that going vegan is about deprivation, because it's not. Check out my Barbarian Torte (page 154) for proof of that.

10 Know that you're not alone. Since being vegan in a non-vegan world is a vast subject, I'll address it more thoroughly in my next book, *Vegan Showgirl Takes Over the World*. For now, I'll say that the social pressure on a vegan surrounded by non-vegans can be daunting. Take heart. Know that you're not alone. Others like you are living this vegan life. Live your heart's convictions and move through the world with compassion and grace. Live from love. That's the Mistress Ginger way. That, and sequins.

STAPLES IN *my pantry*

I just know that you're dying to ask the question, "Mistress Ginger, what's in your panty—I mean, *pantry*?" Well, dears, my panties are invitation only, but my *pantry* is open for all the world to see. Here's a list of my preferred pantry staples, including everything I need to make many a wonderful meal happen on a moment's notice.

Use this list as a reference tool, a template of sorts, a place to start. The world of vegan eats extends far beyond what you see here. Explore the spectrum of what is available and alter or augment this list with seasonal produce, sale items, personal favorites, or the occasional trendy thingamabob. In time, you'll generate your own list of staples composed of your favorite foods to go along with your own unique arsenal of go-to recipes. Stock up, sweetheart!

CONDIMENTS, SEASONINGS, SWEETENERS, AND VINEGARS

agave nectar

brown sugar, light

Coconut Aminos

Dijon mustard

maple syrup

miso (BARLEY, CHICKPEA, AND SWEET WHITE)

molasses

powdered sugar

sea salt

soy sauce, reduced-sodium

sugar, granulated

vegan mayonnaise

vinegar (BALSAMIC, BROWN RICE, CIDER, UME PLUM, WHITE BALSAMIC)

DRIED HERBS AND SPICES

basil

black pepper, whole and ground

caraway seeds, ground

cardamom, ground

cayenne

cinnamon, ground

cloves, ground

coriander, ground

cumin, ground

curry powder

garlic powder

ginger, ground

nutmeg, ground

onion powder

oregano

paprika, ground

parsley

red pepper flakes

rosemary

sage

thyme

turmeric, ground

FRUITS

apples

avocados

bananas

blueberries (FRESH OR FROZEN)

lemons

pears

raisins

GRAINS

bread (WHOLE GRAIN OR MULTIGRAIN)

brown rice

flour (ALL-PURPOSE UNBLEACHED AND WHOLE WHEAT PASTRY)

pasta (WHOLE WHEAT OR GLUTEN-FREE)

quinoa

rolled oats, old-fashioned

LEGUMES

black beans, salt-free canned

chickpeas, salt-free canned

lentils, dried (BROWN, GREEN, RED)

tempeh

tofu (FIRM AND EXTRA-FIRM)

white beans, salt-free canned (CANNELLINI OR GREAT NORTHERN)

NUTS, SEEDS, AND BUTTERS

almonds, raw

cashews, raw

flaxseeds, whole and ground

peanut butter, smooth (NATURAL, UNSWEETENED)

pumpkin seeds, raw

tahini

walnuts

OILS

canola oil

coconut oil

extra-virgin olive oil

toasted sesame oil

vegan buttery spread

VEGETABLES

broccoli

cabbage (GREEN AND RED)

carrots

collard greens

garlic

kale

onions

potatoes

salad greens (LETTUCE OR SPRING MIX)

spinach

winter squash (ACORN OR BUTTERNUT)

yams

ODDS AND ENDS FOR NOW AND THEN

baking powder

baking soda

coconut milk, full-fat canned

Ener-G Egg Replacer

nondairy milk (PLAIN, UNSWEETENED)

nondairy semisweet chocolate chips

nutritional yeast

olives (PITTED KALAMATA OR BLACK)

tomato paste, salt-free

vanilla extract

Useful Utensils and Appliances

Along with having the right foods in your pantry, you'll need to keep the right utensils and appliances handy so you can make the meals of your dreams. Otherwise, you'll just be stirring your batter by hand *with* your hands. While this mess could lead to some fun bedroom shenanigans with the right dinner date, it's not generally advisable for everyday cooking. Now don't get your panties in a bunch if you don't have everything on this list. Just build your collection of kitchen toys as the need arises. In time, you'll have an enviable accumulation of utensils and appliances with which you can create a multitude of mouthwatering meals.

TOOLS OF THE TRADE

baking sheet, nonstick

blender

Bundt pan (9 OR 10 INCHES)

cake pans, round (TWO PANS, EACH 9 INCHES)

casserole dish (6 CUP)

citrus juicer

coffee grinder (USED FOR FLAXSEEDS ONLY)

cooling rack

electric mixer

food processor

loaf pan (8 X 4 X 2½ INCHES)

mixing bowls (VARIOUS SIZES)

mixing spoons, wooden

mortar with pestle

muffin tin (STANDARD, 12 CUP)

pie pan (9 INCHES)

ramekins (SIX, EACH 4½ X 2 INCHES)

rectangular baking pan (13 X 9 INCHES)

saucepans (VARIOUS SIZES, WITH LIDS)

sifter

soup pot (LARGE, WITH LID)

spatulas (METAL AND RUBBER)

springform pan (9 INCHES)

vegetable steamer

whisk

TRICKS OF THE TRADE

- While many of the foods on this list can be stored for weeks or months or even years, others, such as fresh produce, need to be restocked weekly. To ensure that your diet consists mostly of fresh whole foods, make a habit of getting to the grocery store at least once a week—and try to get there when that cute cashier is on the job. You know the one. That curly haired charmer with the scruff and the smile is there every Saturday. A little check-out-line flirtation will enhance the shopping experience, I assure you.

- For optimal health and the most positive global impact, buy organic, seasonal, and locally grown food whenever possible. Go to your local farmers' market and skip around wearing a pink polka-dot sundress with matching parasol.

- Buy produce that has been grown without the use of herbicides and pesticides, even if those farms do not yet have organic certification. Support everyone in the spectrum of do-goodery.

- While most of these foods can be found at a typical supermarket, some items may need to be purchased at a natural food store. If all else fails, you can mail order whatever it is that you need. Google it! If you're lucky, the same suppliers for quinoa will be offering a twofer deal on cruelty-free lip sparkle, and you can have both of these goodies and more mailed to you from one place. Now that's what I call smart shopping!

THOSE FREAKY VEGAN *specialty foods*

Looking over the list of pantry staples on the previous pages, you may have paused once or twice and said to yourself, "What the *freak* is that?" In this glossary of sorts, I define those so-called freak foods, debunk myths associated with them, and share my opinions on how best to use them. Come on now, let's get freaky.

Agave nectar. Agave nectar is a liquid sweetener that's a bit sweeter than honey (bees are animals too, you know!) and thinner in consistency. Extracted from a cactus, agave nectar comes in a spectrum of color, light to dark, with the intensity of the flavor corresponding to the depth of the color. Consisting primarily of fructose, agave nectar is ranked low on the glycemic index, which means it won't spike your blood sugar the way that sucrose sweeteners do.

Chocolate. Chocolate can be vegan, rest assured. Cocoa is naturally vegan and loses its vegan status only when cow's milk is added to it. Read the packaging and opt for fair-trade varieties. (Cocoa butter is vegan, by the way!) I always keep nondairy semisweet dark chocolate chips on hand for those times when Chakra Chip Cookies (page 138) are needed to ease the inner turmoil and set my metaphysical energy centers ablaze.

Coconut Aminos. Coconut Aminos is the brand name of a soy-free, gluten-free seasoning sauce that has a rich, salty flavor. Use it as an alternative to soy sauce or tamari. It's quite lovely.

Ener-G Egg Replacer. Ener-G Egg Replacer is a brand-name product consisting mostly of potato starch and tapioca flour. When mixed with water, it serves as a binding agent in vegan baking. You can whip the egg replacer by hand, but I recommend using a food processor to create a frothy mixture that will most effectively bind your baked goods.

Extra-virgin olive oil. Extra-virgin? Is that even possible? Well, if you're an oil made from olives, it is. Extra-virgin olive oil is deemed to have a taste that's superior to all other grades of olive oil and is best used fresh. "Extra-virgin Mistress Ginger" is a good example of an oxymoron and is a phrase best used to incite rollicking laughter.

Flaxseeds. Flaxseeds are small brown seeds loaded with essential omega-3 fatty acids. To get the recommended daily allowance of omega-3s, eat about two tablespoons of ground flaxseeds a day. Add them to granola, nondairy yogurt, oatmeal, smoothies, and cooked whole grains. Process the flaxseeds in a small coffee grinder (devoted only to grinding flaxseeds) and refrigerate the ground flaxseeds to preserve their nutritional superpowers. To replace one egg as a binder in vegan baked goods, blend 1 tablespoon of ground flaxseeds with 3 tablespoons of water until a viscous mixture is formed. You may also boil whole flaxseeds in water (as I do for the Babooshka Bundles, page 140) to create an egg-white replacer, lovingly referred to as "flax goop."

Hempseeds. Hemp is a highly sustainable crop, and hempseeds are a nutritional powerhouse. They are loaded with omega-3 fatty acids and are a great source of highly digestible protein. Commercially, hempseeds are used to make non-dairy milk, protein powder, and ice cream, among other things. You'll find that Ginger's Balls (page 139) are covered in hempseeds. Though hemp is a variant of the cannabis plant, it doesn't have high levels of the psychoactive ingredients that you would find in that girl Mary Jane, so don't worry (or get your hopes up) that hempseeds will get you high.

Miso. Miso is a traditional Japanese seasoning made by fermenting grains or beans. Miso is available in an array of flavors, ranging from barley, which is darker and saltier, to sweet white, which is sweeter and more mellow. Use barley miso for Hot Mess Dressing (page 121) and lighter chickpea miso for Miso Sexy Soup (page 78). And speaking of Miso Sexy Soup, I recommend using the word "miso" to make declarations about oneself whenever possible. Examples include: miso bootylicious, miso crazy, miso over it, miso all-that-and-a-bag-o-chips, miso in mourning for my lost childhood, and the list goes on. Choose your own adventure. Miso serious.

Nondairy milk. Nondairy milk is milk that has not been squeezed out of a cow's nipple or a giraffe's nipple or any other animal's nipple. The marketplace is booming with an ever-growing variety of milks from plant sources, including almond, coconut, hemp, rice, and soy, to name a few. I recommend buying a fortified unsweetened plain variety, as it can be used for either sweet or savory dishes. I frequently drink soy milk for its satisfying high-protein content and occasionally make my own Angelic Almond Milk (page 50) when I want to feel like an angel. It's the thought that counts.

Nutritional yeast. Nutritional yeast is a deactivated yeast that comes in the form of yellow powder or flakes and imparts a somewhat cheesy flavor. It's a good source of protein and B-complex vitamins, and some vegans swear by the stuff. Among other things, nutritional yeast can be used to add color and flavor to a tofu scramble (see Call-Me-Anytime Scramble, page 29) or a nondairy cheese (see Cheeky Spread, page 122). Nutritional yeast is a highly freaky vegan food, but you'll get over the freak factor in due time. And besides, *le freak, c'est chic!*

Pasta. Let me set your mind at ease. Most pasta is vegan. Though some pasta is made with eggs, it's more often made from just flour, water, and salt. You can find an endless assortment of vegan pastas on the market. Choose a whole-grain variety whenever possible. Note that cooked brown rice pasta may become a little crunchy when chilled and may need to be reheated to be enjoyed as leftovers. For that reason, avoid using brown rice pasta for chilled pasta salad, unless you have a hankering to give your teeth a workout.

Quinoa. Surely you've seen the word "quinoa" floating around the grocery store and wondered what the freak is that. First, let's get the pronunciation right. Repeat after me: KEEN-wah. Very good. Second, let's talk about what it is. It's technically not a grain, but it's like a grain and can be used in your cooking as such. The edible seeds of this grain-like crop can be cooked in just about 15 minutes (see Gorgeous Grains, page 72), and they boast an impressive nutritional profile as a gluten-free source of protein, calcium, phosphorus, fiber, magnesium, and iron. And quinoa is tasty. What more do you need from me, people? I'm unlocking the mysteries of the universe here. Quinoa. Get with the program.

Soy. Soy is not the devil; it's just a bean. You may have heard someone talking trash about the healthfulness of soy. Please, people, stop vilifying this cute little bean! The soybean is a versatile food, a rich protein source, and has been used in vegetarian cooking for thousands of years. Tofu, tempeh, and soy milk are soy foods that have been processed minimally and remain closely linked to their whole-food form, the bean known as edamame. Forms of soy made from soy protein isolate are more processed. Minimize the amount of processed soy that you eat and go for more whole-food versions of the bean. Enjoy soy in moderation, like everything else. Above all, listen to your body, and adjust your soy intake accordingly. Don't be hatin' the soybean.

Tempeh. Tempeh is a fermented soybean cake. Now come back here! It's not as bad as it sounds. This age-old traditional food is a great meat substitute, a good source of protein with a meaty texture. Some people who are sensitive to soy can more easily digest tempeh since it has been fermented. Tempeh must be cooked or steamed to be eaten, and because it's a little bland, it should be cooked with plenty of seasonings and flavor boosters, such as soy sauce or Coconut Aminos. For an easy introduction to tempeh, check out Baba's Tempeh Sandwich (page 86). Before you know it, you will have fallen in love with the fermented soybean cake, and the two of you will be downright inseparable.

Tofu. Like me, tofu is remarkably versatile, like a sponge able to absorb whatever flavor you throw at it. Do throw some flavors at it! Otherwise, in its basic form, tofu is remarkably bland, very much *unlike* me. Available in various textures, from silken soft to super-firm, tofu can be used to create anything from creamy soups to meaty entrées. I prefer an extra-firm variety whenever I want chunks of tofu to withstand being tossed and turned, as in the Flaming Stir-Fry (page 106). I crumble the firm variety to replicate the texture of scrambled eggs in the Call-Me-Anytime Scramble (page 29). Silken tofu can be used as an excellent egg replacer and can be blended into batter to help with binding baked goods, such as Pound-Me Cake (page 152). If ever there were an excuse to try a freaky food like silken tofu, it's to sample something called "Pound-Me Cake." Wouldn't you agree?

MENUS TO FUEL *your fantasies*

Ladies and gents, and everybody else: this is where it's at. The menus! Just as I'm not quite the flawless and lawless showgirl that you've grown to love without an entourage of burly bouncers at my beck and call, a superb main dish is not nearly so spectacular without a throng of sassy side dishes to add complementary flavor, texture, and color. Balancing a meal is an art form, and I'm known to be the Picasso of the plate. Take a lesson from your Mistress: follow a few of these sample menus, and get a taste for how to put together a balanced meal for a breakfast, lunch, dinner, snooty-tooty tea party, or scandalous schmoozefest.

Notice how each of these meals, with the exception of party menus, contains beans, greens, and grains in some form. Also, observe how the textures and colors create beauteous balance on your plate so what you eat can be a feast for your eyes as well as for your tummy. Now, am I a Picasso, or am I a Picasso?

OLD WORLD FEAST

Titillating Tapenade (PAGE 125) on crusty Italian bread

Tomato-Cucumber Carpaccio (PAGE 59)

Mama's Pasta e Fagioli (PAGE 82)

Babooshka Bundles (PAGE 140)

SCANDALOUS SCHMOOZEFEST

Love Juice (PAGE 56)

Mushroom Poppers (PAGE 76)

Potent Pepitas (PAGE 63)

Kickass Guacamole (PAGE 130) with tortilla chips

Ginger's Balls (PAGE 139)

Papa's Potato Candy (PAGE 144)

THE MORNING AFTER

Midnight Pancakes (PAGE 33) with vegan buttery spread and maple syrup

Call-Me-Anytime Scramble (PAGE 29)

Fresh apple slices

Jasmine green tea

TRANSCENDENTAL CHOW

Cosmic Curry Stew (PAGE 84) over Gorgeous Grains (PAGE 72)

Naughty Naan (PAGE 46)

Steamed broccoli

Chakra Chip Cookies (PAGE 138)

ROMANTIC SUPPER FOR TWO (OR MORE)

Threesome Salad (PAGE 58) with Vital Vinaigrette (PAGE 118)

Fit-for-a-Queen Artichokes (PAGE 112)

Valentine Risotto (PAGE 108)

Tie-the-Knot Chocolate–Peanut Butter Pie (PAGE 148)

HIPPIE-DIPPY DINNER

Scarborough Stew (PAGE 79)

Roasted Russell Sprouts (PAGE 64)

Hot Buns (PAGE 44)

Apple-Blueberry Crisp (PAGE 146) with Tenderly Whipped Topping (PAGE 161)

LATIN BINGE-O-RAMA

Buddy's Burrito Bowl (PAGE 115) with Cheeky Sauce (SEE VARIATION, PAGE 122)

Goddess Greens (PAGE 62)

Yam Wedgies (PAGE 70)

Bubbly Bombshell (PAGE 55)

SNOOTY-TOOTY TEA PARTY

Fancy Cucumber Sandwiches (PAGE 94)

Pop-My-Cherry Scones (PAGE 40)

Lemon-Poppy Bundt (PAGE 159)

Vanilla-Nutmeg Chai (PAGE 52)

DETOX ON THE DOWN-LOW

Flaming Stir-Fry (PAGE 106) with Hot Mess Dressing (PAGE 121)

Gorgeous Grains (PAGE 72)

Ginger's Lemon Brew (PAGE 49)

Iced Cocoa Cream (PAGE 160)

In a Flaming Hurry?

The question is, when are we *not* in a flaming hurry? Whatever happened to "be here now?" I think I've replaced it with "I've been there and done that, and I'm going to do it again just to make sure I didn't miss anything the first time."

If you are a hurried flamer like me, consider preparing the side dishes or desserts in advance, or simply use leftovers as a convenient component for a refreshing new meal. Gorgeous Grains (page 72) work especially well in this way since they can be used as a neutral foundation for a variety of splendid dishes, each with its own distinctive flavor and complementary ingredients.

Though you may not always have the time (or the desire) to make four separate dishes for one meal, you can use these menu suggestions as a basic template for creating balance in everyday eats. Also, you are welcome to simplify these menus by "dumbing down" the side dishes. For example, rather than making both Goddess Greens and Yam Wedgies for the Latin Binge-o-Rama, steam some greens and carrots for a similar but much less time-intensive side dish for Buddy's Burrito Bowl. And instead of dressing up the Burrito Bowl with Cheeky Sauce, just add a few avocado slices. The meal will still have a balanced array of flavors, colors, and nutrients to satisfy your deepest cravings and fuel your wildest fantasies.

Come, *cook* with me!

GOOD MORNING, *Sunshine!*

"She was as pure as the driven snow. Then she drifted." Feeling like you've drifted? I know I have (about a hundred times over), and whenever I'm feeling a little out of sorts and in need of purification, I whip up this rawtastic treat, a perfectly smooth blend of tender spinach, fresh fruit, and raw nuts that's bound to purify you, body and soul.

THE GREEN *gulp*

3 tablespoons **raw cashews**

1½ cups **chilled water or coconut water**

1 **fresh or frozen banana**

1 **pear, cut into chunks**

1 cup **spinach, firmly packed**

2 tablespoons **ground flaxseeds**

2 teaspoons **agave nectar**

Put the cashews and water in a blender and process on high speed until smooth. Add the banana, pear, spinach, flaxseeds, and agave nectar. Process until smooth and let the purification commence.

Okay, this smoothie didn't restore you to driven-snow status, but now wasn't that tasty?

Per serving: 453 calories, 15 g protein, 15 g fat (2 g sat), 76 g carbohydrates, 35 mg sodium, 105 mg calcium, 14 g fiber

The lure of the almighty smoothie will swoop you out of bed, and its nutrient-packed essence will give you a lift for the day ahead. In fact, the most challenging thing about having a smoothie for breakfast is deciding how to spend all the time that you just saved by making a smoothie.

SWOOP-ME-UP *smoothie*

1½ cups **plain nondairy milk**

1 **fresh or frozen banana**

½ cup **fresh or frozen berries** (blueberries, strawberries, or raspberries, or a combination)

2 tablespoons **ground flaxseeds**

1 tablespoon **raw cashews or almonds**

2 teaspoons **agave nectar**

Put all the ingredients in a blender and process on high speed until smooth. Sip this through a straw while you paint your toenails, and thank your lucky stars that you bought a blender.

TRICKS OF THE TRADE: If you can't immediately use bananas that have ripened, don't throw them in the trash! Peel the bananas, wrap them individually in plastic wrap (to keep them from sticking together), and put them in a ziplock freezer bag. Store the bananas in the freezer until you're ready to use them.

Not all blenders are powerful enough to blend frozen fruit on a daily basis. Frozen bananas and strawberries are particularly dense and could give your blender a conniption fit if you're not careful. If you don't have an exceptionally high-powered blender (above 700 watts), soak your frozen fruit in warm water for three minutes, drain, and proceed with the recipe with the somewhat softened fruit. Your blender will be so happy that you did.

Per serving: 396 calories, 13 g protein, 13 g fat (1 g sat), 68 g carbohydrates, 231 mg sodium, 499 mg calcium, 10 g fiber

Easiest . . . oatmeal . . . ever. The frozen blueberries quickly thaw in the hot oatmeal and lend a peculiar purple hue to this classic breakfast fare. Purple oatmeal! Have you ever heard of anything more twisted? (Aside from pink hair, of course.)

Twisted OATMEAL

1 cup **old-fashioned rolled oats**

2 cups **water**

Pinch **salt**

½ cup **frozen blueberries**

2 tablespoons **chopped walnuts**

2 tablespoons **ground flaxseeds**

2 tablespoons **maple syrup**

¼ teaspoon **ground cinnamon**

Put the oats, water, and salt in a medium saucepan. Stir until well combined. Bring to a boil over high heat. Remove from the heat and cover. Let sit for 10 minutes. Can you handle this or do you need a private lesson?

Add the blueberries, walnuts, flaxseeds, maple syrup, and cinnamon. Stir gently. Let sit uncovered for 2 to 3 minutes so the blueberries can thaw. Stir once more so the blueberry juice can run amuck in the oatmeal, and serve with a twisted grin on your face.

Per serving: 311 calories, 11 g protein, 11 g fat (1 g sat), 49 g carbohydrates, 8 mg sodium, 66 mg calcium, 7 g fiber

MAKE-IT-YOUR-OWN OATMEAL: Substitute other frozen berries or nuts for the blueberries and walnuts, and modify the proportions to suit your taste and appetite. I don't know about you, but I eat like a bird . . . like a vegan vulture!

TRICKS OF THE TRADE: Save leftovers for a twisted midday snack or for the next day's breakfast.

Apple pie for breakfast? Who could ask for anything more? How about if it's gluten-free and packed with protein? Even better! This creamy porridge makes good use of any quinoa leftovers you have on hand. Simply adjust the proportions of the recipe according to how much leftover quinoa you have, and enjoy your morning dose of apple pie in a bowl.

apple pie PORRIDGE

2 cups **cooked quinoa** (see Gorgeous Grains, page 72)

⅓ cup **raisins**

1¼ cups **water**

1 tablespoon **light brown sugar**

½ teaspoon **ground cinnamon**

⅛ teaspoon **ground nutmeg**

1 **apple, diced**

2 tablespoons **chopped walnuts**

2 tablespoons **ground flaxseeds**

Pinch **ground cinnamon**, for garnish

While your lover sleeps in, slip away to the kitchen. Put the quinoa, raisins, and water in a large saucepan. Stir until well combined. Bring to a boil over high heat. Decrease the heat to medium-low, cover, and simmer until most of the water is absorbed, about 5 minutes. Remove from the heat and let sit covered until the raisins and quinoa are pleasingly plump, about 5 minutes. (This is a good time to brush your teeth and freshen up a bit. Maybe apply a little lipstick. Oh, what the hell, apply a lot of lipstick.)

Put the quinoa mixture into a food processor. Add the brown sugar, cinnamon, and nutmeg. Process several minutes until completely smooth. Add more water if a thinner consistency is desired. (I recommend being in touch with your desires at all times, but especially when you've got a man asleep in the next room.)

Transfer the porridge to serving bowls. Divide the apple, walnuts, and flaxseeds between the bowls and stir to combine. Garnish with the cinnamon and let the fragrant scent of apple pie waft into the bedroom and wake your lover from his restful slumber. Have a quaint breakfast in bed, and then use your gutter-bound imagination for what may follow.

Per serving: 415 calories, 15 g protein, 16 g fat (1 g sat), 60 g carbohydrates, 16 mg sodium, 61 mg calcium, 10 g fiber

In case you haven't heard, those who don dreadlocks and Birkenstocks have been labeled "crunchy," a reference to the crunchy granola that they are reputed to consume by the fistful. Along with that stereotype comes the notion that these "crunchy" people bathe only once a month and avoid wearing sequins at all costs. While that's true for some, this crunchy girl loves her granola as much as she loves her rhinestones. Can't we have it all? With this recipe, we can. Now how did I put the glamour back into granola? With a teaspoon of *Ginger*, of course!

glamola GRANOLA

4 cups **old-fashioned rolled oats**

1 cup **chopped raw nuts**
(walnuts, cashews, or almonds)

½ cup **raw seeds** (pumpkin, sesame, or sunflower)

1 teaspoon **ground cinnamon**

1 teaspoon **ground ginger**

½ teaspoon **salt**

½ cup **maple syrup**

⅓ cup **canola oil**

2 tablespoons **sugar**

2 teaspoons **molasses**

2 teaspoons **vanilla extract**

½ cup **raisins**

Think glam. Preheat the oven to 325 degrees F, and put on your favorite pair of heat-seeking stretch pants.

Put the oats, nuts, seeds, cinnamon, ginger, and salt in a large bowl. Stir until well combined. Put the maple syrup, oil, sugar, molasses, and vanilla extract in a small bowl. Stir with a whisk until well combined. Add the wet mixture to the dry mixture and stir until combined.

Spread the mixture in a 13 x 9-inch baking pan. Bake for 30 minutes, stirring every 10 minutes, until lightly toasted. Remove from the oven, stir in the raisins, and spread the mixture on three or four dinner plates to cool.

Store in a tightly sealed container in the refrigerator. Glamola Granola will keep for 2 weeks.

Look at me, I'm the Mary Poppins for a new age! "Just a teaspoon of ginger helps the granola go glam, the granola go glam, the granola go glam . . ." Well, I'm sort of a deranged Mary Poppins, but a Mary Poppins nonetheless.

Per serving: 472 calories, 10 g protein, 25 g fat (23 g sat), 55 g carbohydrates, 149 mg sodium, 70 mg calcium, 6 g fiber

In the same way that you can call me anytime, you can serve me a tofu scramble anytime: breakfast, lunch, or dinner. Here is a recipe for a simple scramble with classic seasonings. It can be altered according to whatever veggies you have on hand, and leftovers can be reheated or used to make Easy Eggless Egg Salad (see the variation) for that last-minute lunch date with the mailman. Go ahead, serve up this scramble anytime and invite me on over to share it with you (and the mailman). Two's company, but three's a reason to set up the video camera.

CALL-ME-ANYTIME *scramble*

1½ tablespoons **nutritional yeast**

1 teaspoon **salt**

¾ teaspoon **dried parsley**

½ teaspoon **onion powder**

¼ teaspoon **garlic powder**

¼ teaspoon **ground turmeric**

⅛ teaspoon **freshly ground black pepper**

1½ tablespoons **canola oil**

2 cups **vegetables** (see Tricks of the Trade)

1 pound **firm tofu, crumbled**

Mix the nutritional yeast, salt, parsley, onion powder, garlic powder, turmeric, and pepper in a small bowl.

Heat the oil in a medium skillet or saucepan over medium-high heat. Add the vegetables, beginning with the denser vegetables, such as onions and carrots. Cook and stir until somewhat softened, about 3 minutes. Add the lighter or more leafy vegetables, such as broccoli, scallions, and mushrooms. Cook, stirring occasionally, until the veggies are slightly softened, 5 to 10 minutes. You can have the mailman do the stirring if you like.

Decrease the heat to medium and add the tofu and the seasoning mixture. Gently stir until well combined and the tofu turns light yellow.

Cook, stirring occasionally, until the tofu is heated through, about 5 minutes.

Per serving: 244 calories, 20 g protein, 16 g fat (2 g sat), 7 g carbohydrates, 590 mg sodium, 131 mg calcium, 1 g fiber

EASY EGGLESS EGG SALAD: Mix 1 cup of leftover chilled scramble with 2 tablespoons of vegan mayonnaise.

TRICKS OF THE TRADE: For the vegetables, select one or more of the following: broccoli florets, grated peeled carrot, sliced cremini mushrooms, or sliced scallions.

I'm often cooking for my paramours, many of whom prefer it hot and spicy, which is why, of course, they are attracted to me. It's for those sexy spice fiends that I have fashioned this curried scramble. It pairs well with Cha-Cha-Cha Chutney (page 126), which you can spread over some hearty multigrain toast for a breakfast that's sure to get you all hot and bothered (in a good way, I assure you).

hell's kitchen SCRAMBLE

1 cup **chopped onions**

1 tablespoon **minced garlic**

1 tablespoon **canola oil**

½ cup **peeled and grated carrot**

2 teaspoons **curry powder**

¼ teaspoon **ground turmeric**

Pinch **cayenne** (optional)

1 pound **firm or extra-firm tofu**

2 teaspoons **Dijon mustard**

2 teaspoons **reduced-sodium soy sauce or Coconut Aminos**

1½ cups **spinach, lightly packed, coarsely chopped**

Salt

Freshly ground black pepper

Craving something badass in the spice department? You came to the right place. To get started, put the onions and garlic in a food processor and process until smooth.

Heat the oil in a large saucepan over medium-high heat. Add the onion mixture and the carrot and cook until the carrot has softened, about 5 minutes. Add the curry powder, turmeric, and the optional cayenne and cook, stirring constantly, for 1 minute longer.

Crumble the tofu into the pan. Stir until the tofu is evenly mixed with the spices. Stir in the mustard and soy sauce. Decrease the heat to medium and cook until the tofu is heated through, about 5 minutes. Stir in the spinach and cook until the spinach is tender but still bright green, about 2 minutes. Season with salt and pepper to taste, or as requested by your sexy spice fiends.

Per serving: 236 calories, 18 g protein, 15 g fat (3 g sat), 8 g carbohydrates, 217 mg sodium, 149 mg calcium, 1 g fiber

The Wicked Witch of the West has returned, and her gorgeous green glow has inspired these Wicked Waffles, which have a light green hue, compliments of the secret ingredient: spinach! "Oh, what a world, what a world." Serve the waffles with Ruby-Red Syrup (page 134) and you'll likely conjure the spirit of Judy G. herself.

wicked WAFFLES

1⅓ cups **whole wheat pastry flour**

2 teaspoons **baking powder**

2 teaspoons **cornstarch**

½ teaspoon **baking soda**

¼ teaspoon **salt**

1 cup **plain nondairy milk**

¼ cup **spinach, firmly packed**

2 tablespoons **agave nectar**

2 tablespoons **canola oil**

1 tablespoon **sugar**

2 teaspoons **cider vinegar**

½ teaspoon **vanilla extract**

"How about a little fire, Scarecrow?" In other words, preheat a waffle iron.

Put the flour, baking powder, cornstarch, baking soda, and salt in a large bowl. Stir with a dry whisk until well combined.

Put the nondairy milk, spinach, agave nectar, oil, sugar, vinegar, and vanilla extract in a blender and process until even in color and smooth in texture. Pour into the flour mixture and stir to combine.

Spray the waffle iron with nonstick cooking spray. Use about ⅔ cup of batter for each waffle and cook according to the manufacturer's instructions. If you, like me, were given a secondhand waffle iron by a hairy hippie in honor of your second date, then you, like me, won't have the manufacturer's instructions and will just have to do your best to determine how to use this handy appliance. And, like me, you'll wonder why more of your suitors don't gift you with used waffle irons. I can think of nothing sweeter, except perhaps an all-expense-paid trip to Paris in the springtime, but I'll understand if he saves that for the third date.

Per waffle: 395 calories, 7 g protein, 13 g fat (1 g sat), 64 g carbohydrates, 585 mg sodium, 428 mg calcium, 10 g fiber

CLASSIC WAFFLES: Not in the mood for something wicked? For more classically colored waffles, eliminate the spinach and add an additional ¼ cup of nondairy milk.

TRICKS OF THE TRADE: If you can't eat all the Wicked Waffles in one sitting, simply wrap any leftovers in plastic wrap and store them in the freezer until you're good and ready for them. When I'm in a flaming hurry, I just remove the leftover waffles from the plastic wrap and pop them into my toaster oven for a few minutes for a quick breakfast straight from the land of Oz.

Pancakes are the ultimate comfort food, and perhaps the best way to sabotage a low-carb diet. But carb phobes, there's no need to freak out. My pancakes are made with whole-grain flour so you can avoid a colossal blood sugar crash, and these particular pancakes are extra special. The juice from the frozen blueberries spreads into the batter, giving the pancakes a blue-purple hue, like the night sky. It's a perfect midnight snack to fuel a pair of hungry lovers.

midnight PANCAKES

2 cups **whole wheat pastry flour**

2 teaspoons **baking powder**

1 teaspoon **baking soda**

Pinch **salt**

2 cups **plain nondairy milk**

3 tablespoons **sugar**

3 tablespoons **canola oil**, plus more for oiling the skillet

2 teaspoons **vanilla extract**

1⅓ cups **frozen blueberries**

As the clock strikes midnight, preheat the oven to 250 degrees F. It's gotta be midnight somewhere, right? Maybe in Tokyo? (Use that as your excuse to make Midnight Pancakes any time of the day or night.)

In a large bowl, whisk together the flour, baking powder, baking soda, and salt. In a large measuring cup or small bowl, mix the nondairy milk, sugar, oil, and vanilla extract.

Add the wet mixture to the dry mixture. Stir gently until the flour is just moistened. Fold the blueberries into the batter and let sit for about 5 minutes to thicken.

Heat a thin layer of oil in a large skillet over medium heat. Decrease the heat to medium-low and add the batter to the skillet, using a scant ⅓ cup of batter per pancake. (Each pancake will have about a 4½-inch diameter.)

After about 3 minutes, when the pancakes begin to look dry on the edges but still wet in the center and small bubbles form on the tops, flip them to the other side. Have fun flipping your pancakes and see how much air time you can get. (Nine-foot-high ceilings are a must!)

Let the pancakes cook until the other side is golden brown, about 2 minutes, and transfer to a pie pan. Cover the stack with a clean dish towel and put in the oven to keep warm until you're ready to serve.

For subsequent batches, refresh the oil in the skillet as necessary.

Per serving: 136 calories, 4 g protein, 2 g fat (0 g sat), 24 g carbohydrates, 18 mg sodium, 32 mg calcium, 3 g fiber

BANANA BREAD PANCAKES: Omit the blueberries and add 1 cup of chopped banana, ¼ cup of chopped walnuts, and 1 teaspoon of ground cinnamon to the batter.

CHOCOLATE CHIP PANCAKES: Omit the blueberries and add ½ cup of nondairy semi-sweet chocolate chips and 1 additional teaspoon of vanilla extract to the batter.

STRAWBERRY SHORTCAKE PANCAKES: Omit the blueberries and add 1⅓ cups of chopped fresh strawberries to the batter. Serve with maple syrup or Crème Anglaise (page 158).

These delectable crêpes are truly elegant breakfast fare for those mornings when you really want to feel like a classy broad. Go on, put on that floral kimono bathrobe and whip up a batch of these flat French pancakes. Simply divoon, darling, simply divoon! Stuff the crêpes with Coconutty Cream Cheese (page 133), drizzle with Luscious Lemon Syrup, and have yourself a helluva time, even if it is just you and the cats.

 CRÊPES

CRÊPES

1 cup **whole wheat pastry flour**

1½ **tablespoons sugar**

1½ **tablespoons nutritional yeast**

Pinch **salt**

1 tablespoon **ground flaxseeds**

3 tablespoons **water**

1 cup plus 3 tablespoons **plain nondairy milk**

2 tablespoons **canola oil**, plus more for oiling the skillet

FILLING

½ cup **Coconutty Cream Cheese** (page 133)

LUSCIOUS LEMON SYRUP

1 cup **plain nondairy milk**

1 tablespoon **cornstarch**

¼ cup **agave nectar**

1½ tablespoons **freshly squeezed lemon juice**

1 teaspoon **vanilla extract**

Darling peeps, let's make some crêpes. Shall we? Yes, we shall. Whisk together the flour, sugar, nutritional yeast, and salt in a large bowl.

In a small bowl, vigorously whisk together the flaxseeds with the water until the mixture thickens and becomes somewhat frothy. Add the nondairy milk and oil and stir to combine.

Add the wet mixture to the dry mixture. Stir until combined and let sit for 1 minute to thicken.

Lightly coat a medium skillet with oil and heat over medium heat. Add the batter to the skillet, using ½ cup of batter for each crêpe. Tilt the skillet so the batter spreads to create a crêpe about 6 inches in diameter.

After about 3 minutes, when the crêpes begin to look dry on the edges but still wet in the center and small bubbles form on the tops, flip them to the other side. Cook until golden brown and transfer to a pie pan. Cover the stack with a clean dish towel until ready to serve.

For subsequent batches, refresh the skillet with additional oil as necessary.

Getting bored while waiting for your crêpes to cook? Dust off those Julio Iglesias records and dance around the kitchen with your cats. That's what I do.

Now let's make some Luscious Lemon Syrup. Shall we? Yes, we shall. Whisk together ¼ cup of the nondairy milk and the cornstarch until smooth. Combine the remaining ¾ cup of the nondairy milk and the cornstarch mixture and agave nectar in a small saucepan. Bring to a boil over medium-high heat, stirring constantly. Decrease the heat to medium-low and simmer until the sauce thickens. Remove from the heat and stir in the lemon juice and vanilla extract.

To assemble this fancy dish, smear 2 tablespoons of the Coconutty Cream Cheese down the center of a crêpe. Roll the crêpe from one side to the other to enclose the filling. Put the crêpe on a pretty plate and drizzle with the Luscious Lemon Syrup. Oh, dreams do come true.

What is it about the French? They've given us French kissing *and* French toast, two of my favorite things. As I've already perfected the art of French kissing, I thought it high time that I perfected my own version of French toast. Just as the French kiss takes a regular ol' peck on the cheek to the next level, my French-Kissed

french-kissed TOAST

½ cup **plain nondairy milk**

1 tablespoon **cornstarch**

1 tablespoon **ground flaxseeds**

1 tablespoon **sugar**

1 tablespoon **nutritional yeast**

¼ teaspoon **ground cinnamon**

⅛ teaspoon **ground nutmeg**

Pinch **salt**

4 (½-inch-thick) slices **of Bona Fide Banana Bread** (page 41) **or plain sandwich bread** (see Tricks of the Trade)

1½ tablespoons **canola oil**, plus more as needed

Start thinking French, whatever that means to you. Channel Edith Piaf? Wear some French-cut panties? Give your favorite Frenchman a ringy-ding? Or how about all three? That's my vote.

Put the nondairy milk, cornstarch, flaxseeds, sugar, nutritional yeast, cinnamon, nutmeg, and salt in a food processor. Process until the mixture thickens, about 2 minutes, while singing "La Vie en Rose" loud enough to wake the neighbors. Belt it, baby!

Pour the mixture into a small container with a flat bottom, wide enough to fit one slice of bread. Dip each slice of bread in the batter, covering both sides. Let the bread sit in the batter for about 15 seconds to absorb some of the liquid.

Preheat the oven to 250 degrees F.

Heat the oil in a large skillet over medium heat.

Shake the excess batter off the bread and put the slices in the skillet. Cook the bread until browned on one side, about 5 minutes. Flip to the other side and cook until golden brown, about 3 minutes. Transfer to a square cake pan, cover with a clean dish towel, and keep warm in the oven. With the oven on and the kitchen so warm, aren't you glad you decided to wear just your French-cut panties?

Refresh the oil in the pan as necessary for subsequent batches, and stir the batter before coating another slice. Be ready to answer the door at any moment, as François will be arriving soon, just in time to share your French-Kissed Toast and steal some of your French kisses.

Per slice (using Bona Fide Banana Bread): 393 calories, 6 g protein, 20 g fat (2 g sat), 48 g carbohydrates, 319 mg sodium, 121 mg calcium, 6 g fiber

Toast takes run-of-the-mill French toast to the next level. How do I manage that? This breakfast-fantasy-come-true is made using Bona Fide Banana Bread (page 41), bringing another layer of deliciousness to what was already quite delicious. *Bon appétit*, lovers!

TRICKS OF THE TRADE

- French-Kissed Toast is especially good when made with bread that's slightly stale. The dryness allows the bread to soak up more of the batter. If you're using Bona Fide Banana Bread, which is naturally ultramoist, lightly toast the bread before dipping it into the batter.
- If using regular sandwich bread, choose a whole-grain bread that's light in texture and neutral in flavor. Nobody wants French toast made from 16-grain sourdough, or at least I don't think they do. I could be wrong. I hate to admit it, but I was wrong once before, in 1996.

Flapjacks! Pancakes! Griddlecakes! Hotcakes! Whatever you wanna call 'em, I love 'em. I adore pancakes and couldn't resist giving you all my favorite variations: one for every day of the week or for every lover in your little black book. I fashioned this fruit-filled flapjack-fritter hybrid for the truck driver from Chattanooga.

FLAPJACK *fritters*

2 cups **whole wheat pastry flour**

2 teaspoons **baking powder**

2 teaspoons **ground cinnamon**

1 teaspoon **baking soda**

½ teaspoon **ground nutmeg**

¼ teaspoon **ground cloves**

Pinch **salt**

2 cups **plain nondairy milk**

3 tablespoons **sugar**

3 tablespoons **canola oil**, plus more for oiling the skillet

2 teaspoons **vanilla extract**

1⅓ cups **diced peeled apples**

¼ cup **chopped walnuts**

2 tablespoons **raisins**

Tell that trucker to have a seat in your breakfast nook. Give him a cup of tea and a copy of the *Wall Street Journal* to keep him busy while you get to cooking. Preheat the oven to 250 degrees F.

In a large bowl, whisk together the flour, baking powder, cinnamon, baking soda, nutmeg, cloves, and salt. In a large measuring cup or small bowl, mix the nondairy milk, sugar, oil, and vanilla extract.

Add the wet mixture to the dry mixture. Stir gently until the flour is just moistened. (Casually mention to the trucker that your flour has just been moistened.) Fold the apples, walnuts, and raisins into the batter and let sit for 5 minutes to thicken.

Heat a thin layer of oil in a large skillet over medium heat. Decrease the heat to medium-low and add the batter to the skillet, using ⅓ cup of batter per fritter. (Each fritter will have about a 4½-inch diameter.)

After about 3 minutes, when the fritters begin to look dry on the edges but still wet in the center and small bubbles form on the tops, gayly flip them to the other side. Cook until golden brown, about 2 minutes, and transfer to a pie pan. Cover the stack with a clean dish towel and put in the oven to keep warm until serving time.

For subsequent batches, refresh the oil in the skillet as necessary.

Serve up these flapjack-fritter hybrids and have that trucker in the throes of contemplation. "Is this a flapjack or a fritter . . . a flapjack or a fritter . . . a flapjack or a fritter?" He will be deep in thought until you sit on his lap, fan kick over his head, and shake your shimmy in his face. You know, your usual morning routine.

Per serving: 474 calories, 8 g protein, 18 g fat (1 g sat), 71 g carbohydrates, 571 mg sodium, 371 mg calcium, 11 g fiber

BREADS, BEVERAGES, AND A BUBBLY BOMBSHELL

Does the taste and texture of this scone that I've concocted mimic a non-vegan scone exactly? Hell if I know! The truth is, there are so many modern-day varieties of the subtly sweet and buttery biscuits that originated in Scotland, who's to say what's right or wrong? All I know is that if you've never eaten a scone, or even if you have, these cherry-almond scones with a ginger zing are sure to send you reeling into scone heaven, and isn't that where we all want to be?

pop my cherry SCONES

⅓ cup **almond meal**, leftover from Angelic Almond Milk (page 50), or ⅓ cup **unbleached all-purpose flour**

1⅔ cups **whole wheat pastry flour**

1 tablespoon **baking powder**

1 teaspoon **baking soda**

¼ teaspoon **ground ginger**

¼ teaspoon **salt**

⅓ cup **vegan buttery spread**

1 tablespoon **Ener-G Egg Replacer**

¼ cup **warm water**

½ cup **maple syrup**

1 teaspoon **vanilla extract**

½ teaspoon **almond extract** (optional)

¾ cup **chopped pitted fresh cherries**

½ cup **sliced almonds**

3 tablespoons **diced crystallized ginger**

1 tablespoon **sugar**

Preheat the oven to 400 degrees F. Put on your most ruffly apron and lightly oil a baking sheet or line it with parchment paper.

Put the almond meal, flour, baking powder, baking soda, ground ginger, and salt in a large bowl. Stir with a dry whisk until well combined. Using a fork or pastry blender, cut in the vegan buttery spread until the flour is moistened and pea-sized crumbs have formed, each about the size of the diamond that's on my finger.

Put the egg replacer and water in a food processor and process until frothy, about 3 minutes. Add the maple syrup, vanilla extract, and optional almond extract. Process until smooth, stopping as needed to scrape down the work bowl with a rubber spatula.

Stir the wet mixture into the dry mixture with a wooden spoon. When just mixed, fold in the cherries, almonds, and crystallized ginger.

Drop eight ⅓-cup mounds of batter onto the prepared baking sheet. Using your hands, shape each mound into a triangle, about ¾ inch thick. (But be sure to wash your hands first. Lord only knows where they've been. Well, you and the cable guy also know.)

Sprinkle the triangular mounds evenly with the sugar.

Bake for about 12 minutes, until golden brown. Transfer to a cooling rack and let cool for at least 5 minutes before serving. Serve warm and give everyone a taste of your ginger zing.

Scones can be stored for 1 week in a tightly sealed container in the refrigerator.

Per scone: 308 calories, 5 g protein, 13 g fat (3 g sat), 43 g carbohydrates, 432 mg sodium, 205 mg calcium, 5 g fiber

This banana bread is the real deal. The flavor is subtly sweet, and the texture is magically moist. Hmm, sweet and moist, just like a little nibble of yours truly. Made with whole-grain flour and chock-full of nuts, this wonderfully wholesome loaf can serve as either a healthy dessert or a decadent snack. For an extra-special breakfast or brunch, use Bona Fide Banana Bread to make an outrageous batch of French-Kissed Toast (page 36). Amazeballs!

BONA FIDE *banana bread*

YIELDS 1 LOAF, 8 SERVINGS

1½ cups **whole wheat pastry flour**, plus more for flouring the pan

1 teaspoon **baking powder**

¼ teaspoon **baking soda**

¾ teaspoon **ground cinnamon**

¾ teaspoon **salt**

1½ cups **mashed bananas** (about 3 very ripe bananas)

⅓ cup **canola oil**

¼ cup **maple syrup**

¼ cup **light brown sugar**, firmly packed

1 teaspoon **vanilla extract**

½ cup **chopped walnuts**

Preheat the oven to 350 degrees F. Lightly coat a 9 x 5-inch loaf pan with vegetable shortening. Sprinkle with flour and then shake and tap out the excess. (This shaking and tapping could spontaneously erupt into an elaborate song and dance. That kind of thing doesn't only happen in old movies. It also happens in Ginger's kitchen.)

Put the flour, baking powder, baking soda, cinnamon, and salt in a large bowl. Stir with a dry whisk until well combined.

Put the bananas, oil, maple syrup, brown sugar, and vanilla extract in a food processor and process until smooth.

Add the wet mixture to the dry mixture. Stir until combined. Fold in the walnuts. Pour the batter into the prepared pan and bake for 50 minutes, or until a toothpick inserted in the center comes out clean. Let cool for at least 2 hours before slicing, and then do a happy dance because this banana bread is finally ready for your nibbling pleasure.

To store, tightly wrap the cooled loaf in plastic wrap and keep in the refrigerator. Finish off this subtly sweet and magically moist loaf within 1 week. I don't think that will be a problem.

Per serving: 308 calories, 4 g protein, 14 g fat (1 g sat), 41 g carbohydrates, 300 mg sodium, 77 mg calcium, 5 g fiber

These delicately spiced pumpkin muffins are studded with dried blueberries. I encourage you to feed them to your personal entourage of stud muffins as part of a bountiful breakfast or midday snack. Try these muffins with a schmear of Coconutty Cream Cheese (page 133) for an especially luscious stud-muffin experience, something I'm always up for.

BLUEBERRY *stud muffins*

YIELDS 12 MUFFINS

2 cups **whole wheat pastry flour**

2 teaspoons **baking powder**

2 teaspoons **ground cinnamon**

½ teaspoon **baking soda**

¼ teaspoon **ground nutmeg**

¼ teaspoon **salt**

⅛ teaspoon **ground cloves**

⅛ teaspoon **ground ginger**

1 cup **pumpkin purée**

½ cup **maple syrup**

½ cup **vanilla nondairy yogurt**

⅓ cup **canola oil**

¼ cup **sugar**

1 teaspoon **vanilla extract**

½ cup **dried blueberries**

Preheat the oven to 350 degrees F. Lightly oil a twelve-cup muffin tin or line it with paper stud-muffin cups.

Put the flour, baking powder, cinnamon, baking soda, nutmeg, salt, cloves, and ginger in a medium bowl. Stir with a dry whisk until well combined.

Put the pumpkin purée, maple syrup, nondairy yogurt, oil, sugar, and vanilla extract in a large bowl. Stir with a whisk until well combined.

Add the dry mixture to the wet mixture and stir to combine. Fold in the blueberries.

Pour the batter into the prepared muffin cups, filling each cup completely.

Bake for 20 to 25 minutes, until a toothpick inserted in the center of a muffin comes out clean. Let the muffins rest in the muffin tin for about 5 minutes before transferring to a cooling rack. Serve warm or at room temperature.

Blueberry Stud Muffins will stay fresh for up to 1 week when stored in a tightly sealed container in the refrigerator. Your personal entourage of stud muffins will stay fresh as long as they wear a good cruelty-free deodorant and bathe at least once a day. I'm prepared to assist with the bathing.

Per muffin: 209 calories, 3 g protein, 7 g fat (1 g sat), 35 g carbohydrates, 163 mg sodium, 122 mg calcium, 4 g fiber

PUMPKIN-RAISIN STUD MUFFINS: Imagine that you just ran out of dried blueberries but are dying for some hot stud-muffin action. Simply substitute the dried blueberries with ½ cup of raisins. Problem deliciously solved.

CHOCOLATE STUD MUFFINS: What? You've never had a chocolate stud-muffin experience? Oh, darling, you're missing out! Substitute the dried blueberries with ½ cup of nondairy semisweet chocolate chips and cross "chocolate stud-muffin experience" off your bucket list.

I can hear it now. "Ginger, wasn't 'Savor Me Muffin' your nickname back in high school?" What? How could you think such a thing? That's ridiculous. My nickname was never "Savor Me Muffin." It was *"Juicy Muffin!"* A Savor Me Muffin is actually just a savory muffin, a faux-cheesy, fresh-herby, comfort-foody concoction that will send you into fits of ecstasy and unbridled abandon. Okay, I can see where you got confused.

savor me MUFFINS

1 cup **whole wheat pastry flour**

½ cup **cornmeal**

1½ teaspoons **baking powder**

¾ teaspoon **salt**

½ teaspoon **baking soda**

1 tablespoon **Ener-G Egg Replacer**

3 tablespoons **warm water**

½ cup **plain nondairy milk**

¼ cup **canola oil**

3 tablespoons **chopped fresh chives**

2 tablespoons **minced fresh parsley**

2 tablespoons **chilled Cheeky Spread** (page 122)

Are you ready to savor me muffins? Well, hop to it, hot stuff. Preheat the oven to 350 degrees F. Lightly oil six cups of a muffin tin or line them with paper muffin cups.

Put the flour, cornmeal, baking powder, salt, and baking soda in a large bowl. Stir until well combined.

Put the egg replacer and water in a food processor and process for 3 minutes, until frothy. Frothy, I said!

In a small bowl, whisk together the nondairy milk, oil, and egg replacer mixture.

Add the wet mixture to the dry mixture. Mix until just combined. Fold the chives and parsley into the batter.

Put about 2 tablespoons of batter into each of the six prepared muffin cups. Put about 1 teaspoon of Cheeky Spread in the center of each mound of batter. Divide the remaining batter among the six cups to cover the Cheeky Spread completely. The Cheeky Spread will be the creamy gem in the center of your crusty muffin. ("Creamy Gem" was also one of my high school nicknames, but I'm glad to report that "Crusty Muffin" was not.)

Bake for 15 minutes, until golden brown. Let sit in the pan for 3 to 5 minutes to cool slightly. Transfer to a cooling rack and let cool for at least 10 minutes longer before serving and savoring.

Savor Me Muffins should be stored in a tightly sealed container in the refrigerator and savored within 1 week.

Per muffin: 220 calories, 3 g protein, 10 g fat (1 g sat), 28 g carbohydrates, 532 mg sodium, 171 mg calcium, 3 g fiber

I've been told that I have the best buns in town, and now word has gotten out. Everybody wants to try my buns. I get people banging on my bedroom window in the middle of the night. "Let us try your buns!" Just last week, a busload of Greek sailors stopped by, all of them eager to try my buns. What

 BUNS

¼ cup **hot water** (110 to 115 degrees F)

1 (¼-ounce) **package active dry yeast**

2 tablespoons plus ½ teaspoon **sugar**

2½ cups **unbleached all-purpose flour**, plus more for kneading the dough

½ cup **plain unsweetened nondairy milk**

2 tablespoons **vegan buttery spread**, softened

½ teaspoon **salt**

1 teaspoon **dried rosemary, partially crushed** (optional)

Let's get down to business, the business of baking buns, which is very serious business indeed. To begin, put the hot water in a measuring cup. I recommend using hot tap water and testing it with a food thermometer to make sure that it's the right temperature. The right temperature is very important, almost as important as a good-quality eyelash glue. (Never leave home without it!)

Put the water, yeast, and ½ teaspoon of the sugar in a large bowl. Gently stir to combine and let the mixture sit until it foams and doubles in size, about 10 minutes.

Add 1 cup of the flour, the nondairy milk, vegan buttery spread, salt, and optional rosemary to the yeast mixture. Using an electric mixer, blend until smooth. Add another cup of the flour and mix again until well incorporated and a thicker dough forms. Add the remaining ½ cup of the flour, 1 tablespoon at a time, just until a soft dough forms.

Knead the dough for 2 to 3 minutes on a lightly floured countertop.

Lightly coat a medium bowl with vegetable shortening. Put the dough ball in the bowl and roll it around until lightly coated. Cover the bowl with a clean dish towel and let sit in a warm, draft-free place until the dough has doubled in size, about 1 hour. While you wait, choreograph an interpretive dance using my hot buns and the rising of the dough as inspiration.

Preheat the oven to 375 degrees F. Lightly coat a 9-inch round cake pan with vegetable shortening.

Now, to get all your aggressions out, punch down the dough. (Exercise a little caution here. The last time I did this, I damn-near bruised a knuckle.) Divide the dough into nine balls. Arrange the balls in the prepared pan, evenly spaced from each other and the sides of the pan.

can I say? My buns are damn tasty, and even tastier when you spread my buns with a little nondairy butter—I mean, when you spread a little nondairy butter on my buns. Either way, I'll have you burnin' up for my buns.

Bake for 20 to 25 minutes, until gorgeously golden brown. (This is the only time you'll hear me say that I've got a bun in the oven. Knock on wood.)

Remove from the oven and let sit in the pan on a cooling rack for 5 minutes. Remove from the pan and let your Hot Buns cool for at least 5 minutes longer before serving. Everyone will want to bite into your buns while they're still hot. Tell them to wait, that your buns are too hot to handle, that they'll enjoy your Hot Buns much more once they've cooled slightly, as paradoxical as that may seem.

Store leftover buns in a tightly sealed container in the refrigerator and use within 1 week. Reheat leftover Hot Buns before eating. Wrap them in foil and warm for 5 minutes in an oven preheated to 250 degrees F. I know a million and one *other* ways to warm up a pair of cold buns, but those I'll have to teach you when my overhead projector is back from the shop.

Per bun: 159 calories, 5 g protein, 3 g fat (1 g sat), 28 g carbohydrates, 162 mg sodium, 25 mg calcium, 1 g fiber

You go to an Indian restaurant, and boohoo! You can't eat the bread because it was made with ghee, also known as clarified butter. Who the hell needs clarified butter? The only thing that needs clarified around here is this: butter is utterly unnecessary! You will soon realize this for yourself once you take a bite of my Naughty

 NAAN

¾ cup **plain nondairy milk**

1 (¼-ounce) **package active dry yeast**

1 teaspoon **sugar**

2 cups **unbleached all-purpose flour**, plus more for rolling the dough

1½ cups **whole wheat pastry flour**

1 teaspoon **salt**, plus more for sprinkling

2 tablespoons **coconut oil**, plus more for oiling the skillet

1¼ cups **finely chopped onions**

1 cup **plain nondairy yogurt**

Heat the nondairy milk in a small saucepan over medium-low heat until hot but not boiling, 110 to 115 degrees F. I recommend using a food thermometer to take the temperature of the nondairy milk (and it sure will come in handy the next time you're playing doctor).

Put the warm nondairy milk, yeast, and sugar in a small bowl. Let sit until the mixture begins to foam like a rabid dog, about 10 minutes.

Put the all-purpose flour, whole wheat pastry flour, and salt in a large bowl and stir with a dry whisk to combine.

If the coconut oil has solidified, heat it in a small saucepan over low heat to liquefy and let cool to room temperature. Add the oil, onions, and nondairy yogurt to the yeast mixture. Stir to combine.

Add the wet mixture to the dry mixture and stir until a sticky dough is formed.

Knead the dough on a lightly floured countertop, adding flour as necessary to keep the dough from sticking, for about 5 minutes. Quit your complaining! Maybe the exercise will do you some good. Just thank your lucky stars that you're not a rabid dog.

Lightly oil the dough ball, cover with plastic wrap, and let sit in a warm, draft-free place until doubled in size, about 1 hour.

Punch down the dough. (This is my favorite part! I so rarely get to punch anything without worrying that it'll punch back.)

Divide the dough into ten pieces. Roll each piece into a ball and wrap each ball with plastic wrap. (Optionally, at this point the ten dough balls can be chilled for up to four hours before proceeding with the recipe.) Let sit for 10 minutes.

Naan, made naughty with a touch of the Mistress. Yes, it takes a little time to roll out the dough. Cry me a river, sweetheart! You'll soon get over it. I've not only given you an alternative to naan, I've given you an upgrade. So stop your whining and start thanking me for bringing naan back into your life.

Lightly coat a large skillet with oil and heat over medium heat.

On the lightly floured countertop, roll out each piece of dough into an oval, about ⅛ inch thick. Use extra flour to prevent sticking. Sprinkle the dough with salt.

Put the oval dough in the pan and cook until puffed up and golden brown in spots, about 3 minutes on each side.

Refresh the oil in the pan as necessary for subsequent batches.

Put the cooked naan on a plate and cover with a clean dish towel to keep warm until it's time to eat. You may be tempted to nibble on some Naughty Naan before dinner is ready, but then your Mistress would have to give you a good old-fashioned spanking. Something tells me that you wouldn't mind those consequences, you naughty, naughty nibbler.

Store leftover naan in a tightly sealed container in the refrigerator and use within 1 week.

Per piece: 206 calories, 6 g protein, 4 g fat (2 g sat), 38 g carbohydrates, 245 mg sodium, 55 mg calcium, 4 g fiber

Keep those annoying teenage vampires away with this ultra-garlicky garlic bread, and serve it up alongside Lip-Smackin' Lasagna (page 104) or Mama's Pasta e Fagioli (page 82). Or, if you don't believe in vampires (which I think you'd be taking your chances not to), you can just serve this bread around twilight time, as the sun goes down and the candles are lit for that romantic dinner for two, three, or maybe eight.

Twilight GARLIC BREAD

⅓ cup **vegan buttery spread, softened**

2 tablespoons **finely minced garlic**

1 tablespoon **minced fresh parsley,** or 1 teaspoon dried

1 (20-inch) **French baguette**

Preheat the oven to 350 degrees F. Though you might be a tad warm, do *not* remove that pink chiffon scarf. Protect that exquisite neck at all costs. Trust me, fang marks aren't a good look for you.

In a small bowl, combine the vegan buttery spread, garlic, and parsley. Be sure that the smell of garlic is wafting out the window as a clear warning to any thirsty succubae strolling down the street.

Cut the round ends off the baguette. Then cut the baguette in half to create two smaller pieces, each about 8 to 10 inches long. Cut each piece in half lengthwise.

Spread the garlic mixture evenly on the cut side of each of the four bread pieces. Put the buttered sides together to form two small loaves and wrap both loaves in aluminum foil. Put both loaves on a baking sheet.

Bake for 15 minutes, until good and toasty. Are you getting warm? Spritz yourself with a little holy water. Just don't remove that scarf, unless you wanna spend your afterlife on the prowl after dark. (Of course, many of you are already accustomed to prowling after dark.)

Remove from the oven, unwrap, and lay the four bread pieces on the foil cut-side up. Bake for 3 to 5 minutes longer.

Remove from the oven. Rewrap in the foil until ready to serve. FYI, should someone try to get all vampirical on your ass, a loaf of garlic bread wrapped in foil can double as a stake through the heart.

Per serving: 147 calories, 2 g protein, 8 g fat (2 g sat), 13 g carbohydrates, 198 mg sodium, 0 mg calcium, 1 g fiber

Ginger and lemon are a couple of Mother Nature's magic ingredients with healing properties that have been noted throughout the ages. (In this instance, I am speaking of ginger *root*, not *Mistress* Ginger, though it's fair to say that I too am some kind of force of nature.) Heated, this brewed lemon juice and ginger root will warm you up on a cold winter day. Chilled, it refreshes like lemonade, perfect in the blazing heat of summer.

GINGER'S *lemon brew*

YIELDS 2⅓ CUPS, 2 SERVINGS

2 cups **water**

1 tablespoon **peeled and minced fresh ginger**

¼ cup **freshly squeezed lemon juice**

2 tablespoons **agave nectar**

Put the water and ginger in a small saucepan and bring to a boil over high heat. Decrease the heat to medium-low and simmer for 5 minutes. You'll notice that ginger root loves to simmer just as Mistress Ginger loves to shimmer.

Remove from the heat. Pour through a fine-mesh strainer set over a large measuring cup or small bowl. Add the lemon juice and agave nectar and stir to combine.

Serve my healing brew warm or chilled and spend the remainder of the day shimmering in your eternal gorgeousness.

Per serving: 66 calories, 0 g protein, 0 g fat (0 g sat), 18 g carbohydrates, 3 mg sodium, 2 mg calcium, 0 g fiber

I'm no angel, believe me. I've been there, done that, and did it again, just to make sure I didn't miss anything the first time. Nonetheless, I bring you this almond milk straight from heaven. Pour this liquid love over a bowl of Glamola Granola (page 28) or just drink it straight up. I swear, my third eye just

angelic ALMOND MILK

½ cup **raw almonds, soaked in water for 6 to 8 hours**

4 cups **water**

2 tablespoons **maple syrup or agave nectar**

2 teaspoons **vanilla extract**

¼ teaspoon **ground cinnamon**

Let's begin with those precious almonds. Pop the skins off 'em. Discard the skins (or put them in your scrapbook, the one titled "Everything I Need to Know I Learned from Mistress Ginger").

Put the naked almonds and 2 cups of the water in a blender and process on high speed until smooth, about 1 minute.

Now stick with me, folks. I will attempt to describe how you can strain your almonds to achieve the smoothest almond milk in the history of the world. Rest a fine-mesh strainer over the mouth of a large glass measuring cup or small bowl. Double a piece of cheesecloth, forming a square large enough to cover the strainer. In half-cup batches, pour the almond mixture through the cheesecloth and strainer. Let the liquid drain into the bowl or measuring cup. When the liquid stops draining, gather the sides of the cheesecloth around the mixture and tightly squeeze the cheesecloth so the remainder of the liquid pours through the strainer. Unwrap the cheesecloth and transfer the residual pulp (aka almond meal) to a small bowl. Repeat with the remaining almond mixture.

Have I lost ya? Oh, good. You're still there. You'll be relieved to know that that was the hard part. Now we breeze our way to the finish line.

Rinse the blender and pour the strained liquid back into it. Add the remaining 2 cups of the water and the maple syrup, vanilla extract, and cinnamon. Blend for another 30 seconds and transfer to a large jar or pitcher. Chill before serving.

opens up when I take a swig of this stuff. Sure, it takes a little extra time to prepare, but it's worth it (for a shortcut, see *In a flaming hurry?* below). You'll go from sinner to saint with one sip.

Sip and feel the earth move under your six-inch platform heels. Store in a tightly sealed container in the refrigerator and use within 1 week for all your purifying needs.

Per serving (not strained): 119 calories, 4 g protein, 7 g fat (1 g sat), 10 g carbohydrates, 0 mg sodium, 52 mg calcium, 2 g fiber

Per serving (strained): 111 calories, 4 g protein, 7 g fat (1 g sat), 8 g carbohydrates, 0 mg sodium, 52 mg calcium, 0 g fiber

TRICKS OF THE TRADE

- The leftover almond meal can be used in baked goods, such as Pop-My-Cherry Scones (page 40).
- For a thicker almond milk, use more almonds or less water to achieve the desired consistency.

In a flaming hurry?

Omit the straining process. The resulting almond milk won't be as smooth, but it will still be almond milk and will still send you straight to heaven in a handbasket.

Don't these words sound like music to your ears, making you think of a brisk autumn afternoon roaming the city, arm in arm with the loved one of your choice, stopping into a quaint coffee shop and grabbing one of those spicy teas, and then sipping your way to heart-melting warmth, snuggling and cooing, just before he pops the big question: "What's your name?" Oh, details, details! Now you can learn to make this heart-warming chai at home and have a good excuse to ask him back to your place.

VANILLA-NUTMEG *chai*

YIELDS 5¼ CUPS, 5 SERVINGS

4 cups **water**

8 **cardamom pods**

8 **whole cloves**

8 **peppercorns**

2 **cinnamon sticks**

1 whole **nutmeg**

½ **vanilla bean**, sliced lengthwise

3 bags **black tea**

1½ cups **plain nondairy milk**

2 tablespoons **light brown sugar**, firmly packed

Ground nutmeg, for garnish

"Would you like to come back to my place? I make a wonderful chai . . ." Once he's inside, lock the doors, close the blinds, and pull out your big saucepan. Put the water, cardamom pods, cloves, peppercorns, cinnamon sticks, whole nutmeg, and vanilla bean in the saucepan. Bring to a boil over high heat. Cover, decrease the heat to medium-low, and simmer for 5 minutes. Remove from the heat and let sit covered for 10 minutes. (These steeping times are great opportunities to fondle your beloved, whatever his name is.)

Uncover the saucepan and bring to a boil over high heat again. Remove from the heat. Add the tea bags, cover, and let steep for 3 to 5 minutes. (Again, fondling time.)

Remove the tea bags. Add the nondairy milk and brown sugar. Warm over low heat until heated through, about 5 minutes. Strain through a fine-mesh strainer into mugs and sprinkle individual servings with ground nutmeg. Serve in the privacy of your own home, where you and your anonymous other can do as you like.

Store leftover chai in a tightly sealed container in the refrigerator and use within 1 week.

Per serving: 38 calories, 0 g protein, 1 g fat (0.1 g sat), 8 g carbohydrates, 51 mg sodium, 90 mg calcium, 0 g fiber

ICED CHAI LATTE: Those fancy coffee shop drinks can be yours, sans the fancy price tag. Chill that bad boy in the fridge, throw in a few ice cubes, and voilà!

When you're in need of refreshment, run, don't walk, to your nearest citrus juicer. Juice a couple of grapefruits, pour the juice into a glass, add a few complementary ingredients, and then lounge in your favorite caftan, sipping your way to sublime refreshment.

BUBBLY *bombshell*

1 cup **freshly squeezed ruby-red grapefruit juice** (about 2 ruby-red grapefruits)

1½ tablespoons **freshly squeezed lime juice**

2 cups **sparkling water, chilled**

2 tablespoons **agave nectar**

Simply strain the grapefruit and lime juice through a fine-mesh strainer into a serving pitcher. Chill until ready to serve. Just before serving, add the sparkling water and agave nectar and stir. Toss a little umbrella or swizzle stick into each glass, just for good measure.

As you sip your sparkling beverage, ponder one of the great existential questions of eternal time and space: Is the Bubbly Bombshell that which is sipped or the one who sips? Profound, I know.

Per serving: 49 calories, 0 g protein, 0 g fat (0 g sat), 11 g carbohydrates, 89 mg sodium, 6 mg calcium, 0 g fiber

You can think of this special drink as your love potion number 451. You'll need that many love potions, one for every occasion, or for every Greek sailor, however you'd like to count them. Homemade cherry juice is the centerpiece of this spritely virgin cocktail. What? Did I say "virgin"? Oh, I guess I did. But I'm including a non-virginal option as well. Truly, at this point, non-virginal is my only option.

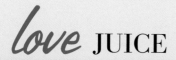

love JUICE

2 cups **pitted fresh or frozen cherries**

4 cups **water**

2 cups **apple juice**

2 cups **sparkling water**

1 tablespoon **agave nectar**

¾ cup **Kirsch** (optional; see Tricks of the Trade)

6 **fresh cherries with stems,** for garnish

Wherever you fall in the spectrum of virginity, put the cherries and water in a large saucepan and bring to a boil over high heat. Decrease the heat to medium-low and simmer uncovered for 30 minutes.

Remove from the heat and let sit in the pan until cooled to room temperature. Strain the cherry juice through a fine mesh strainer into a serving pitcher. Refrigerate for at least 30 minutes.

Once you've got all your guests assembled and eagerly awaiting some love in the form of juice, you may proceed.

Add the apple juice, sparkling water, and agave nectar to the cherry juice and stir. To prepare each serving, put 3 or 4 ice cubes in a 2-cup drinking glass. Add 2 tablespoons of the optional Kirsch and 1 cup of the juice mixture and stir. With a dramatic flourish, drop a fresh cherry into each glass.

I recommend wearing something low cut and cherry red when you serve this drink, just to drive the point home. What's the point? Oh, if you have to ask, it doesn't matter anymore.

Per serving: 104 calories, 1 g protein, 0 g fat (0 g sat), 25 g carbohydrates, 7 mg sodium, 1 mg calcium, 0 g fiber

TRICKS OF THE TRADE: Also called *Kirschwasser*, German for "cherry water," Kirsch is a brandy made from cherries. That's right, boys and girls, hold on to your hairnets; we're talking about alcohol. It's not sweet, but it does taste a bit like cherries with a hint of bitter almond. Boozers beware—less is more in the case of Kirsch. I know you'll be tempted, but don't chug the stuff like you're at one of your weekly keggers. Instead, lace your Love Juice with just a hint of cherry brandy, or use it to make my heaven-sent Strawberry Short-cake (page 158). I think of Kirsch as the perfect spirit to take my spirits to the moon and back.

SALADS, SIDES, AND LITTLE LOVE BITES

You can choose from an endless variety of veggies to make a raw salad, but here is my staple salad, which offers a balanced array of textures and colors from ingredients I almost always have in my fridge. These three vegetables offer a satisfying trifecta of color and flavor and texture—a threesome, if you will. Give this threesome a whirl. There's a first time for everything.

Threesome SALAD

5 cups **spring lettuce mix, lightly packed**

½ cup **shredded red cabbage**

1 **carrot, peeled and grated**

Toss the vegetables together in a medium serving bowl. However will you recover from this backbreaking effort?

Per serving: 27 calories, 2 g protein, 0 g fat (0 g sat), 5 g carbohydrates, 54 mg sodium, 51 mg calcium, 2 g fiber

TRICKS OF THE TRADE: It's fun to play around with different threesomes now and then. Consider the other dishes you're serving at the meal and choose vegetables that add complementary variety in terms of color, flavor, and texture. Here are some additional threesomes you can try:

- Baby arugula, peeled and chopped cucumber, and chopped red bell pepper
- Bibb lettuce, sliced zucchini, and grated beets
- Romaine lettuce, shredded radicchio, and cherry tomatoes

Another way to spice up a threesome salad (aside from making it a foursome) is to add a delicious dressing, and as your Mistress, I absolutely demand that you splash some creamy concoction over your threesome. I recommend Vital Vinaigrette (page 118), Mistress Ginger Dressing (page 119), Drizzle Me Dressing (page 120), or any of your favorite salad dressings, store-bought or homemade. Make this threesome yours!

The success of this classy summer salad relies on the quality of your ingredients. Fresh vegetables are a must. Also, the olive oil and balsamic vinegar are showcased, and their distinctive flavors take this dish to the next level of taste-bud bliss. Nothing says summer like garden-fresh tomatoes and cucumbers, except, of course, for my itsy-bitsy, teeny-weeny, yellow polka-dot bikini. Now there's a visual for you to sink your teeth into!

TOMATO-CUCUMBER *carpaccio*

CAPER DRESSING

2 tablespoons **balsamic vinegar**

1 tablespoon **extra-virgin olive oil**

1 tablespoon **capers, rinsed**

1 tablespoon **minced red onion**

½ teaspoon **dried basil**

¼ teaspoon **minced garlic**

Pinch **salt**

CARPACCIO

1 **cucumber**

3 **tomatoes**

Freshly ground **black pepper**

To make the dressing, put the vinegar, oil, capers, onion, basil, garlic, and salt in a small bowl or measuring cup. Whisk with a fork until well combined. Let sit for at least 15 minutes, until the flavors have become entwined like the limbs of a couple of leggy lovers locked in heavenly transport.

While the flavors are entwining, prepare the carpaccio. Peel and slice the cucumber into ¼-inch-thick rounds (about twenty slices). Slice the tomatoes into ¼-inch-thick rounds (about ten slices).

On a large plate or serving platter, arrange a single layer of the cucumber slices. Over the cucumber, create a second layer with the tomato slices.

Drizzle the dressing over the vegetables and sprinkle with pepper to taste. Behold, the carpaccio is complete! Hello? Are you there? Or are you still spellbound by the thought of me in my bikini? I realize that I have planted a most indelible image in your mind, but snap out of it! Time to eat.

Per serving: 66 calories, 1 g protein, 4 g fat (1 g sat), 8 g carbohydrates, 72 mg sodium, 24 mg calcium, 2 g fiber

TRICKS OF THE TRADE: Like me, Caper Dressing can liven up any meal. Use it on your favorite vegetable or grain salad or substitute it for other dressings in this book.

Picture it: a steamy, sultry, summer day in the land of Ginger. My air conditioner is on the fritz, and I'm all hot and bothered (but *not* in good way). I'm sweatin' up a storm with my mascara running a marathon and my coif frizzed out to Fargo and back. I can't bear to cook. No, I want something fresh and raw. And here it is: a giant salad, just for me. This vegetable bonanza can serve as an entire meal for one hottie, or it can be divided into a number of hearty side salads to accompany a multicourse meal for multiple hotties.

mondo SALADE

3 cups **spring lettuce mix, lightly packed**

¾ cup **shredded kale**

¾ cup **shredded red cabbage**

½ cup **peeled and grated carrot**

½ cup **chopped red bell pepper**

½ cup **small broccoli florets**

2 tablespoons **chopped red onion**

2 tablespoons **raisins**

1 tablespoon **raw pumpkin seeds or sunflower seeds**

¼ cup **Drizzle Me Dressing** (page 120) or other dressing

It's getting hot in here.

Option one: Take off all your clothes.

Option two: Put the spring lettuce mix, kale, cabbage, carrot, bell pepper, broccoli, onion, raisins, and pumpkin seeds in a large bowl. Drizzle with the dressing. Toss until the dressing evenly coats all the ingredients, and serve (yourself).

Hmm . . . tough call. I choose option three, all of the above!

Per serving: 369 calories, 15 g protein, 16 g fat (4 g sat), 49 g carbohydrates, 756 mg sodium, 171 mg calcium, 6 g fiber

TRICKS OF THE TRADE: When I make this enormous salad, I put the veggies directly into a six-cup storage container or casserole dish. I drizzle the dressing over the veggies, cover the container with a tight-fitting lid, and shake it. Shake it, sister! Shake what your mama gave ya! And once you're done shaking it, you'll find that the salad is evenly coated with dressing and that your cats are staring at you in bewilderment.

VARIATIONS: What? More options? The ingredients listed above are only the tip of the iceberg. Use your favorite veggies or just what you happen to have on hand. Other potential add-ins include beans, blueberries, cauliflower, edamame, green peas, radish, spinach, strawberries, tamari-seasoned almonds, walnuts, cooked tempeh (see Baba's Tempeh Sandwich, page 86), or Tofu Gone Wild (page 75).

Kale is the new ice cream. Really, it's gotten such good press in the last few years that you'd think it was junk food. Brimming with vitamins and low in calories, kale is hard to beat in the realm of nutrient-dense foods. Here is an easy, not sleazy, preparation for the superstar leafy green.

emerald city KALE

1 tablespoon **toasted sesame oil**

5 cups **kale, rinsed and chopped into bite-sized pieces**

1 tablespoon **reduced-sodium soy sauce or Coconut Aminos**

2 teaspoons **raw or roasted sesame seeds**

1 teaspoon **brown rice vinegar**

How do I get to Emerald City Kale? Follow the yellow brick road? I don't think so, girlfriend. I don't do cobblestones in these six-inch heels.

I have a better idea. Heat the oil in a large skillet over medium-high heat. Add the kale (a little wet from having been rinsed). Cook, stirring frequently, until the kale is tender but still bright green, 5 to 10 minutes. Stir in the soy sauce and cook until most of the liquid evaporates, 2 to 3 minutes longer. Remove from the heat, stir in the sesame seeds and vinegar, and you've arrived.

Per serving: 81 calories, 3 g protein, 5 g fat (1 g sat), 9 g carbohydrates, 229 mg sodium, 123 mg calcium, 2 g fiber

I am psycho—I mean psychic—and I know what you're thinking: "Ginger, was this recipe named after you?" But of course! I am divine, just as your greens will be divine once you smother them with a tangy avocado dressing. Then, when you put them in your mouth, you'll think of me, goddess that I am.

goddess GREENS

3 cups **chopped kale or collard greens, lightly packed**

½ **ripe avocado**

1½ tablespoons **freshly squeezed lemon juice**

1 tablespoon **extra-virgin olive oil**

2 teaspoons **minced onion**

¼ teaspoon **minced garlic**

Pinch **salt**

I see tender kale dressed with tangy cream sauce in your future, but you must begin at the very beginning. Like the goddess Julie Andrews said, it's a very good place to start.

Steam the kale until bright green, about 5 minutes. Transfer to a medium bowl.

To prepare the dressing, put the avocado, lemon juice, oil, onion, garlic, and salt in a food processor and process until well blended.

Toss the dressing with the warm greens.

Put individual servings in small bowls or on plates alongside the main dish. Serve these greens with full awareness of the goddess in you.

Per serving: 180 calories, 4 g protein, 13 g fat (2 g sat), 16 g carbohydrates, 44 mg sodium, 141 mg calcium, 5 g fiber

VARIATION: Sometimes the goddess wants to go raw. To create a dressing with a thinner consistency for a raw vegetable salad, combine the avocado, lemon juice, oil, onion, garlic, and salt with 1 tablespoon of water and 1 additional teaspoon of lemon juice.

In a flaming hurry?

Goddess on the go? Don't make a dressing at all. Instead, slice the avocado and arrange it over the steamed greens, drizzle with lemon juice, and sprinkle with a pinch of salt.

Sometimes you have to stoke a man's fire to get him interested, and I've been called the human blowtorch. But I can't take all the credit. Many of the foods that I feed to my lovers are known to boost libido. Case in point: Potent Pepitas. I conveniently provide a small bowl of these spiced pumpkin seeds as a pre-dinner snack for my dates. Before I know it, the spicy seeds are gone, and my date wants to skip dinner and go directly to dessert. This is not a problem.

POTENT *pepitas*

¼ teaspoon **ground cumin**

¼ teaspoon **garlic powder**

¼ teaspoon **ground paprika**

¼ teaspoon **salt**

Pinch **cayenne**

1 cup **raw pumpkin seeds**

2 teaspoons **extra-virgin olive oil**

1 teaspoon **liquid smoke**

Combine the cumin, garlic powder, paprika, salt, and cayenne in a small bowl. Think of it like a magic potion.

Toast the pumpkin seeds in a dry medium skillet over medium heat, stirring frequently, until puffed up and lightly browned. Remove from the heat and spread on a plate to cool.

Warm the oil in the skillet over medium heat. Add the seasoning mix and stir constantly for about 20 seconds. Add the pumpkin seeds and liquid smoke and toss gently until the seeds are completely coated and any liquid has evaporated, about 1 minute.

Transfer the seeds to a plate lined with a paper towel to soak up the excess oil and let cool to room temperature. Transfer to a small bowl, and when your lover arrives, serve these babies up.

Save leftover Potent Pepitas in a tightly sealed container in the fridge and use within 2 weeks. If your social calendar is anything like mine, finishing up your Potent Pepitas within a couple of weeks won't be an issue. In fact, you may need to make a new batch every other day.

Per ¼ cup: 184 calories, 8 g protein, 17 g fat (0.3 g sat), 6 g carbohydrates, 145 mg sodium, 0 mg calcium, 1 g fiber

I once made Brussels sprouts for a guy named Russell, and a night of unbridled passion ensued. I name this dish in honor of him, and in honor of the fits of ecstasy that he threw me into. Roasted or sautéed, Brussels sprouts have the potential to be crispy, creamy nuggets of love. This simple preparation

ROASTED RUSSELL *sprouts*

20 **Brussels sprouts,** similar in size, ends trimmed lengthwise, and cut in half (about 2½ cups)

2 tablespoons **olive oil**

½ teaspoon **caraway seeds,** crushed in a mortar with pestle

½ teaspoon **salt,** plus more as needed

1 tablespoon **minced garlic**

Freshly ground **black pepper**

Inquiring (and oversexed) minds want to know, "How does one get thrown into a fit of ecstasy?" Start by turning up the heat. In plain terms, preheat the oven to 400 degrees F.

Mix the Brussels sprouts with 1½ tablespoons of the oil and the caraway seeds and salt. Arrange the Brussels sprouts on a baking sheet, cut-side up. Roast in the oven for 13 to 15 minutes, until just tender. Remove from the oven and sprinkle with the garlic and the remaining ½ tablespoon of the oil and stir. Turn the Brussels sprouts over so the cut sides face down. Roast 3 to 5 minutes longer, until the garlic becomes fragrant. Transfer immediately to a serving dish.

Season with additional salt and pepper to taste. Be warned—your dinner guests may experience fits of ecstasy right there at the table. There's no telling whose toes may twitch, whose back may arch, or what expletives will fly in the heat of the moment once they sink their teeth into these succulent nuggets of love.

Per serving: 201 calories, 6 g protein, 15 g fat (2 g sat), 17 g carbohydrates, 615 mg sodium, 83 mg calcium, 6 g fiber

includes expert tips on how to roast the Brussels sprout to sumptuous perfection, thus priming you and your beloved for a night of passion replete with fits of ecstasy.

TRICKS OF THE TRADE

- This recipe could easily feed just one or two people. Double the recipe if you plan on serving more than one hungry lover.

- I specify arranging the Brussels sprouts cut-side up initially because they will be easier to turn over and it will be easier to keep track of which sprouts have been roasted on which side. This way, you can achieve a more evenly cooked bunch of sprouts. Also, if the round side should become burnt and blackened (and if you're not fond of blackened sprouts), you can simply remove those outer leaves before serving. Aren't I brilliant?*

The correct answer is "Yes, Mistress, you are brilliant . . . brilliant and breathtaking."

Oh, broccoli naysayers, beware! This dish will get you to call off all bets. You won't be able to resist the rich dressing, the exotic spice blend, or the avalanche of cranberries and peanuts that will carry your taste buds away to Morocco, where swarthy guys with bronzed pectorals are spooning this creamy concoction into your mouth. Seriously now, how can you decline an invitation to be transported and spoon-fed?

moroccan BROCCOLI

4 cups **broccoli, cut into small florets**

¾ cup **silken tofu**

2 teaspoons **extra-virgin olive oil**

2 teaspoons **freshly squeezed lemon juice**

¾ teaspoon **salt**

⅛ teaspoon **ground ginger**

⅛ teaspoon **ground cumin**

⅛ teaspoon **ground paprika**

⅛ teaspoon **ground turmeric**

⅛ teaspoon **ground cinnamon**

⅓ cup **dried cranberries**

¼ cup **unsalted roasted peanuts, coarsely chopped**

Beam me up, Morocco! Steam the broccoli just until bright green and still crisp, about 3 minutes. Remove from the heat, transfer to a medium serving bowl, and chill.

To prepare the dressing, combine the tofu, oil, lemon juice, salt, ginger, cumin, paprika, turmeric, and cinnamon in a food processor. Process for several minutes until smooth, stopping as needed to scrape down the work bowl with a rubber spatula.

To assemble the salad, combine the chilled broccoli with the dressing. Stir in the cranberries and peanuts and chill until you are ready to be transported to Morocco. Bring on the bronzed pectorals!

Per serving: 169 calories, 7 g protein, 8 g fat (1 g sat), 20 g carbohydrates, 457 mg sodium, 62 mg calcium, 4 g fiber

Once upon a time, I was a strictly macrobiotic showgirl who used a minimum of added seasonings and sweeteners in her natural food cookery. One of my favorite macrobiotic dishes was nishime (pronounced nish-EEM-ee). My version of this traditional Japanese vegetable stew reveals the inherent sweetness of the

CABBAGE PATCH *nishime*

3-inch piece **dried kombu** (optional)

3 **carrots, peeled and cut into 1-inch pieces** (about 1 cup)

½ small **unpeeled winter squash, cut into 1-inch pieces** (about 2½ cups)

1 small **onion, cut into 1-inch pieces** (about 1½ cups)

¼ small **green cabbage, cut into 1-inch pieces** (about 2 cups)

¾ cup **water**

1 tablespoon **reduced-sodium soy sauce or Coconut Aminos**

Craving the antithesis of gas-station cuisine? You've come to the right showgirl.

Put the kombu, if using, in a small bowl. Cover with water and let soak for about 5 minutes. Drain and cut the kombu into 1-inch pieces and put in a large saucepan.

Layer the vegetables over the kombu, starting with the carrots, then the squash, then the onion, then the cabbage.

Add the water and bring to a boil over high heat. Decrease the heat to medium, cover, and simmer until the vegetables are very tender, about 15 minutes.

Add the soy sauce, cover, and shake the saucepan gently. Simmer until all the vegetables are soft and beginning to disintegrate, about 5 minutes.

Serve and let these sweet vegetables just melt in your mouth. You will wonder, "How long has this been going on? Healthy has never tasted so good." Oh, yes it has. These foods have been around for eons. You just didn't know about them, but better late than never.

Per serving: 71 calories, 3 g protein, 1 g fat (0.1 g sat), 16 g carbohydrates, 231 mg sodium, 35 mg calcium, 5 g fiber

cabbage, carrot, onion, and squash. The stew is very low in fat and calories, but you wouldn't know it. Slow cooked, the veggies become sweet, soft, and creamy, leading you back for guilt-free second helpings and curbing your cravings for a sugary dessert. Eat your nishime, and you might just live happily ever after.

TRICKS OF THE TRADE: Since the only added seasoning in this dish is the soy sauce, you'll taste the distinctive flavor of whatever brand you choose. Shoyu soy sauce and traditional tamari have deep, rich flavors, but both are high in sodium. If you opt for one of these varieties, use it sparingly and savor it completely.

VARIATIONS

- Use other root vegetables if you wish. Replace the winter squash with yam. Throw parsnip or daikon radish into the mix. What the hell, add a little minced ginger or garlic.
- To transform this recipe into a main dish, toss in some chickpeas or other beans during the last 5 minutes of cooking, or add the cooked tempeh (cubed) from Baba's Tempeh Sandwich (page 86). To make this veggie stew stick to your ribs, drizzle it with a little Hot Mess Dressing (page 121) or the peanut sauce from the Peanut-Pea Pasta (page 116).

Oh, my beloved yam, I could write you a love poem. "Roses are red, violets are blue, yams are sweet, and nutritious too. How do I love thee? Let me count the ways. One, two, three, four . . . Oh, I could go on for days. Shall I compare thee to a French fry? Hardly, for thou art more orange and more sweet." Then I hear you say, "Oh, Mistress Mine, don't be such a tease. Just roast me in the oven at 350 degrees." Will do.

YAM *wedgies*

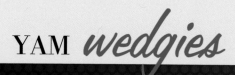

2 tablespoons **extra-virgin olive oil**

¼ teaspoon **salt**

¼ teaspoon **onion powder**

⅛ teaspoon **garlic powder**

⅛ teaspoon **freshly ground black pepper**

⅛ teaspoon **cayenne** (optional)

2 pounds **yams, peeled and cut into wedges** (about 4 x ¾ inches)

Wax poetic and preheat the oven to 375 degrees F.

Here's my ode to the humble yam:

Put the oil, salt, onion powder, garlic powder, pepper, and optional cayenne in a small bowl. Stir until well combined and sing to the mate of your soul.

In a large bowl, drizzle the oil mixture over your darling yam. Stir until those yams are thoroughly coated and all you can say is . . . hot damn!

Arrange the yams in a single layer on a nonstick baking sheet. Bake for 20 to 30 minutes, turning the yams every 10 minutes so they absorb the heat.

While the yams bake, write at least three more yam-centric songs. When the yams are tender and golden brown, transfer them to a plate using a pair of tongs.

Okay, I'm no Wordsworth, but you get the picture.

Per serving: 326 calories, 4 g protein, 7 g fat (1 g sat), 63 g carbohydrates, 163 mg sodium, 39 mg calcium, 9 g fiber

You might think that I'm out of my mind to put this ridiculously simple recipe in a cookbook, but remember that this book is not only intended for you savvy cooks; it's also for those who have been grabbing their grub at the local Pump-N-Munch. Whole grains are a vital component of a healthy diet,

gorgeous GRAINS

1½ cups **whole grains**

3 cups **water**

Pinch **salt**

Screw on your bedazzled thinking caps because the utter complexity of this recipe method is bound to blow your mind.

Mix all the ingredients in a medium or large saucepan. Bring to a boil over high heat, cover, decrease the heat to medium-low, and simmer until no water is left in the saucepan. (See the variations that follow for approximate cooking times.) Turn off the heat and let sit covered for 10 minutes. Uncover, fluff with a fork, and serve.

Unless you plum forgot about this dish and burned the hell out it, I don't think there's a chance you could have screwed it up. But if you did, you'll get no judgment from Ginger. I'll just suggest that you get your thinking cap re-bedazzled. (It's sort of like being born again, but for showgirls.)

Per serving (using quinoa): 255 calories, 8 g protein, 2 g fat (0 g sat), 45 g carbohydrates, 25 mg sodium, 30 mg calcium, 6 g fiber

NOTE: Nutritional information will vary based on the choice of grains.

TRICKS OF THE TRADE: This isn't brain surgery. There are essentially two types of whole grains: the denser, slow-cooking kind and the lighter, quick-cooking kind. The wild and wonderful world of grains includes many unique varieties. Explore the spectrum and keep things interesting, just as you do with that endless parade of lovers you've got trickling from your boudoir.

Keep the ratio of water to grains 2:1. The recipe above yields about 3 cups of grains, which is enough for 3 to 4 servings. Of course, you can always make more or less, depending on your needs. Hosting another dinner party for the Croatian soccer team? I recommend tripling this recipe and

and they're easy to make. When you have the time, make a large batch of grains and then use the leftovers to prepare quick meals later in the week. That's the Mistress Ginger way. That, and sexy see-through nighties.

supplementing the meal with my Hot Buns, and some dinner rolls (page 44) would be nice too.

SLOW-COOKING GRAINS: Dense grains need to cook for 45 to 50 minutes. Any sort of brown rice fits into this category. For me, short-grain brown rice is truly a staple food, but long-grain brown rice is especially good in the summer. Other grains in this category include barley, buckwheat, and rye, which can be cooked alone or mixed with brown rice. For instance, use 1 cup of short-grain brown rice with ½ cup of pearled barley.

QUICK-COOKING GRAINS: Lighter grains need to cook for only 15 to 20 minutes. "What? Whole grains in only fifteen minutes? I don't believe it!" Well, believe it, baby. It's true. My favorite quick-cooking grain is quinoa (pronounced KEEN-wa; see page 15), which is an excellent source of high-quality protein. Then there's millet, which I sometimes mix with quinoa (see Quinoa-Millet Pilaf, page 98) or cook by itself. You gas-station connoisseurs, you have no more excuses. Whole grains can be yours in a flash.

I acquired my love for these hash-brown nuggets down at the local fire station. After CPR classes (for which I was the volunteer dummy), the firefighters and I would sit around eating these fiery morsels like they were going out of style. I let the guys throw them into my mouth from across the room, and on special occasions they slurped them like body shots from my ample cleavage. Okay, maybe I'm exaggerating a little. My cleavage is not ample, but these tots are hot! So invite some of your local firefighters over to slurp these bad boys from your own cleavage. And for a really hot mess, dip the tots in ketchup or Cheeky Spread (page 122).

 TOTS

YIELDS 6 HOT TOTS, 3 SERVINGS

1 pound **russet potatoes, peeled and grated** (about 2 cups)

¾ teaspoon **salt**

¼ cup **diced red bell pepper**

1½ tablespoons **canola oil**, plus more for oiling the pan

1 tablespoon **cornstarch**

½ teaspoon **onion powder**

¼ teaspoon **garlic powder**

¼ teaspoon **ground paprika**

Pinch **cayenne**

Freshly ground **black pepper**

Preheat the oven to 375 degrees F. Oil six cups of a nonstick muffin tin. Get a few firefighters to help you with oiling the tin and see where that leads.

If you haven't gotten completely sidetracked, put the grated potatoes and salt in a medium bowl. Stir until well combined.

In half-cup batches, put the potato mixture in a paper towel and squeeze out the excess liquid. (You will probably need to use a new piece of paper towel for every batch.) Put the drained potato mixture in a separate medium bowl. Add the bell pepper, oil, cornstarch, onion powder, garlic powder, paprika, cayenne, and black pepper to taste. Stir until well combined.

Squeeze ⅓ cup of the potato mixture in your hand to remove more excess liquid if possible and press into a prepared muffin cup. Continue until all six cups are filled about ½ inch deep.

Bake for 30 minutes. While the tots are baking, the firefighters can take turns giving you rubdowns.

Flip the tots over and bake for 5 minutes longer, until golden brown on both sides.

Per serving: 193 calories, 3 g protein, 7 g fat (1 g sat), 30 g carbohydrates, 578 mg sodium, 20 mg calcium, 2 g fiber

TRICKS OF THE TRADE: Hot Tot body shots should be executed at your own risk (and for your own pleasure).

"Flavor-packed tofu, and no marinating required? It can't be!" Oh, yes it can, and I wouldn't have it any other way. Who's got the time for marinating? Not I, not after a long day of whirling, twirling, and general show-girling. I'm sure you can relate. Don't you just feel like a runaway disco ball on the dance floor of life? And don't you just come home after a long day at the jamboree wanting a one-way ticket to tasty tofu that you can throw on a Threesome Salad (page 58), into Peanut-Pea Pasta (page 116), or alongside some simple grains and greens? I thought so. Now permit me to teach you how to infuse bland cubes of tofu with wowsa flava in an instant. Hold on to your bobby pins, boys and girls, because this tofu has gone wild!

TOFU *gone wild*

1½ tablespoons **canola oil**

1 pound **extra-firm tofu, cubed**

1 teaspoon **onion powder**

½ teaspoon **garlic powder**

¼ teaspoon **ground paprika**

⅛ teaspoon **dried thyme**

½ teaspoon **freshly ground black pepper**

1½ tablespoons **reduced-sodium soy sauce or Coconut Aminos**

Heat the oil in a large skillet over medium-high heat. Add the tofu and cook, stirring occasionally, until lightly browned on all sides, about 10 minutes.

While the tofu cooks, mix the onion powder, garlic powder, paprika, thyme, pepper, and soy sauce in a small bowl. Spice is nice, like paradise.

Once the tofu is browned, add the soy sauce mixture and cook, stirring constantly, until all the liquid evaporates, about 2 minutes.

Transfer the tofu to a plate lined with a paper towel to soak up the excess oil.

Enjoy your Tofu Gone Wild warm or chilled. Store leftovers in a tightly sealed container in the refrigerator, use within 1 week, and by all means, go wild.

Per serving: 235 calories, 19 g protein, 16 g fat (3 g sat), 4 g carbohydrates, 310 mg sodium, 141 mg calcium, 0 g fiber

These baked mushroom caps stuffed with Nottaricotta (page 132) are the perfect finger food for your next scandalous schmoozefest. Be warned, your guests will linger around the refreshment table just so they can keep popping these juicy morsels into their mouths. To get their attention, you'll have to do something outrageous, like sitting in the kitchen sink, bawling your eyes out while singing "Proud Mary" at the top of your lungs. I just throw this out there as a hypothetical scenario. This never actually happened, and you can't prove that it did.

mushroom POPPERS

¾ cup **Nottaricotta** (page 132)

3 tablespoons **diced kalamata olives**

1 teaspoon **freshly squeezed lemon juice**

20 large **cremini mushrooms**

1 tablespoon **extra-virgin olive oil**

¼ teaspoon **salt**

Pinch **freshly ground black pepper**

Before you've got your party people in the house, preheat the oven to 375 degrees F. Lightly oil a baking sheet or line it with parchment paper. Wear something to remind your guests that, no matter how good these stuffed mushrooms are, you are the most succulent morsel in town by far.

Put the Nottaricotta in a small bowl. Add the olives and lemon juice and mix well.

Remove the stems from the mushrooms. Wipe the mushrooms clean with a damp paper towel.

Combine the oil, salt, and pepper in a medium bowl. Spread the oil mixture evenly around the inside of the bowl. Add the mushrooms to the bowl and toss gently until lightly coated.

Fill each mushroom cap with about 2 teaspoons of the Nottaricotta mixture (depending on the size of the caps). The filling should be mounded. Arrange the caps on the prepared baking sheet, filling-side up.

Bake for 15 minutes, until the filling begins to lightly brown. Let cool for at least 10 minutes before serving.

If you aim to keep your guests' undivided attention, be prepared to commence a song-and-dance extravaganza immediately upon serving these succulent morsels. I bet you never thought you'd be competing with a stuffed mushroom for affection, but all I can say is that desperate times call for desperate measures. Not that I'm desperate. These Mushroom Poppers are just that good.

Per popper: 34 calories, 2 g protein, 3 g fat (0.1 g sat), 1 g carbohydrates, 49 mg sodium, 21 mg calcium, 0 g fiber

SOUPS, STEWS,
AND SULTRY SANDWICHES

Me so sexy. You so sexy. We so sexy. Feeling better now? No? Well, if it's more than a communal ego boost you're seeking, have a steaming bowl of my marvelous miso soup. I've concocted this vegan version of chicken soup with some truly healing ingredients. Loaded with greens, beans, and grains, this hearty soup can serve as a potent one-pot meal that'll help you feel like your sexy self again in no time flat.

miso sexy SOUP

2 cups **salt-free cooked or canned chickpeas, rinsed and drained**

1 cup **chopped onions**

½ cup **peeled and diced carrot**

¼ cup **diced celery**

1½ tablespoons **minced garlic**

1½ tablespoons **minced fresh parsley, or 1 teaspoon dried**

1 tablespoon **peeled and minced fresh ginger**

4 cups **salt-free vegetable broth**

4 cups **water**

2 cups **cooked brown rice** (see Gorgeous Grains, page 72)

2 tablespoons **chickpea miso**

¼ cup **nutritional yeast**

3 cups **chopped kale** (cut into bite-sized pieces)

The time has come for me to sex you up. To begin, I'll have you put the chickpeas, onions, carrot, celery, garlic, parsley, ginger, broth, and water in a large soup pot. Bring to a boil over high heat. Decrease the heat to medium-low, cover, and simmer for 15 minutes. Add the rice, cover, and simmer until heated through, about 5 minutes.

Scoop ¼ cup of the broth into a small bowl. Add the miso and whisk until the miso dissolves.

Add the miso mixture, nutritional yeast, and kale to the pot. Let the soup simmer until the kale is tender, at least 5 minutes. Get to slurping and feeling sexy.

Miso glad we had this time together.

Per serving: 349 calories, 15 g protein, 3 g fat (1 g sat), 69 g carbohydrates, 336 mg sodium, 146 mg calcium, 11 g fiber

This hearty lentil stew derives its name from the use of those four lovely herbs: parsley, sage, rosemary, and thyme (found in the lyrics of the folk song "Scarborough Fair" that Simon and Garfunkel made famous in the sixties). I considered calling this dish "Garfunkel Stew" but then thought not. The word "funk" shouldn't be permitted anywhere near something so savory and scrumptious as this.

SCARBOROUGH *stew*

- 1 tablespoon **extra-virgin olive oil**
- 1½ cups **chopped onions**
- 1 tablespoon **minced garlic**
- 4 cups **salt-free vegetable broth**
- 1½ cups **carrots, peeled and cut into 1-inch pieces**
- 1½ cups **potatoes, peeled and cut into 1-inch pieces**
- 1 cup **dried brown lentils, rinsed and drained**
- 2 **bay leaves**
- 1 teaspoon **dried parsley**
- ½ teaspoon **dried sage**
- ½ teaspoon **dried rosemary**
- ½ teaspoon **dried thyme**
- ¾ teaspoon **salt**
- Freshly ground **black pepper**

Listen up, flower children and hipsters alike. Whether you're decked out in bell-bottoms or skinny jeans, heat the oil in a large soup pot over medium-high heat for 30 seconds. Add the onions and cook, stirring frequently, until soft and translucent, about 5 minutes. Add the garlic and cook, stirring frequently, for 1 minute.

Add the broth, carrots, potatoes, and lentils and bring to a boil over high heat.

Add the bay leaves, parsley, sage, rosemary, and thyme. Decrease the heat to medium, cover, and simmer for 45 minutes, stirring occasionally. While you wait, pull out the guitar and serenade me with "Mr. Bojangles."

Add the salt and season with pepper to taste. Simmer uncovered until most of the broth is absorbed or evaporates, about 15 minutes. Remove the bay leaves before serving.

Make stew, not war.

Per serving: 149 calories, 8 g protein, 2 g fat (0.3 g sat), 32 g carbohydrates, 330 mg sodium, 37 mg calcium, 10 g fiber

TRICKS OF THE TRADE: To become the mistress of your own culinary domain, start with adapting soups and stews such as this one. Think of this recipe as a template and freely alter the proportions or the ingredients to suit your taste. Just keep the ratio of liquid to beans and veggies about the same to ensure that you have adequate liquid to fully cook them. Once you're familiar with how this recipe works, you can add more or less broth for a thinner or thicker consistency. You'll be the dominatrix of your kitchen. Now all you need are some thigh-high black boots and an apron fashioned from fishnet.

I've brazenly borrowed some of the flavors and textures that we commonly associate with seafood dishes, and I've done them up all fancy-like. I don't normally go for gourmet stuff like this. Believe it or not, I'm more of a peasant-food type of gal. Give me a pile of lentils in a clay pot, and I'm good to go. However, every

brazen BUTTERNUT BISQUE

1 large **butternut squash,
peeled and cut into 1-inch pieces**
(about 5 cups)

1 large **onion, coarsely chopped**
(about 2 cups)

6 cups **water**

1½ tablespoons **extra-virgin
olive oil**

3 cups **coarsely chopped
shiitake mushrooms**

1 teaspoon **Old Bay Seasoning**

Salt

2 teaspoons **toasted sesame oil
or extra-virgin olive oil**

½ teaspoon **ground paprika**

Parsley sprigs, for garnish

I don't usually recommend cooking in a billowing Balenciaga gown, but in this case I do, just to get you in the right frame of mind.

Once you're dressed to the nines, put the squash, onion, and water in a large soup pot. Bring to a boil over high heat. Decrease the heat to medium, cover, and simmer until the squash and onion are very tender, about 30 minutes.

While the squash and onion cook, prepare the mushrooms. Heat the oil in a large skillet over medium-high heat. Add the mushrooms and cook until softened, 5 to 7 minutes. Remove from the heat and stir in the Old Bay Seasoning. Transfer to a small bowl and set aside. The long satin gloves might get a little messy here. As always, carry a spare pair.

Once the squash and onion have cooked, remove from the heat and let sit for 5 minutes to cool slightly. Twirl while you wait. (The dress will be crying out for it.)

Discard 2 cups of liquid from the squash mixture. In 1-cup batches, process the remaining squash mixture in a food processor until smooth. Put each processed batch in a large saucepan and stir to combine.

Put the saucepan on the stove and heat over medium heat. Season with salt to taste.

Put the sesame oil and paprika in a small bowl and stir to combine.

now and then, one has to do dinner deluxe. This squash soup has few ingredients and a simple preparation, but the artful presentation will have your guests falling all over themselves just to say in their backwater drawl, "You is so fancy!" You can thank them (and correct their grammar later).

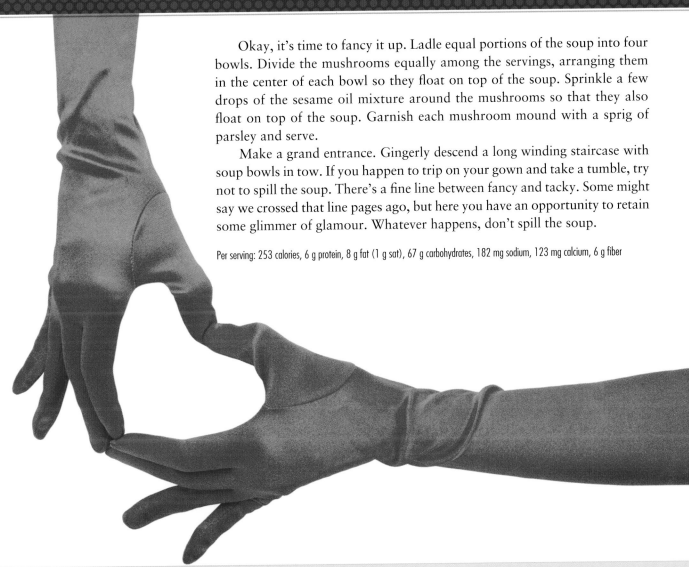

Okay, it's time to fancy it up. Ladle equal portions of the soup into four bowls. Divide the mushrooms equally among the servings, arranging them in the center of each bowl so they float on top of the soup. Sprinkle a few drops of the sesame oil mixture around the mushrooms so that they also float on top of the soup. Garnish each mushroom mound with a sprig of parsley and serve.

Make a grand entrance. Gingerly descend a long winding staircase with soup bowls in tow. If you happen to trip on your gown and take a tumble, try not to spill the soup. There's a fine line between fancy and tacky. Some might say we crossed that line pages ago, but here you have an opportunity to retain some glimmer of glamour. Whatever happens, don't spill the soup.

Per serving: 253 calories, 6 g protein, 8 g fat (1 g sat), 67 g carbohydrates, 182 mg sodium, 123 mg calcium, 6 g fiber

This creamy soup has a special place in my heart. It's just like Mama used to make, except that I replace the chicken broth with vegetable broth. Many of our beloved foods are already vegan or nearly so. I prefer to make this soup more like a stew by adding less of the optional pasta cooking liquid. The creamy goodness flavored with pungent garlic and divine rosemary makes for the ultimate comfort food. *Bellissimo!*

mama's PASTA E FAGIOLI

2 tablespoons **extra-virgin olive oil**

½ cup **peeled and diced carrot**

2 tablespoons **minced garlic**

4 cups **salt-free vegetable broth**

4 (15-ounce) cans **salt-free great Northern beans, rinsed and drained**

2 tablespoons **salt-free tomato paste**

2 tablespoons **dried rosemary, crushed**

12 ounces **pasta** (medium shells or orecchiette)

Salt

Freshly ground **black pepper**

Lovers of Italian cooking unite! (And lovers of Italian descent give me a call.) Heat the oil in a large soup pot over medium-high heat for 30 seconds. Add the carrot and cook, stirring frequently, until beginning to soften, 3 to 5 minutes. Add the garlic and cook, stirring frequently, for 1 to 2 minutes. Add the broth, beans, tomato paste, and rosemary. Increase the heat to high and bring to a boil. Decrease the heat to medium and cook uncovered for 30 minutes. (A guy named Giovanni actually did just call. He said he'd like to come over for dinner.)

While the bean mixture cooks (and Giovanni is on speakerphone), prepare the pasta. Before draining, be sure to set aside 2 cups of the pasta water. Drain and rinse the pasta.

Stir the pasta into the bean mixture, dilute with the pasta water to the desired consistency, and season with salt and pepper to taste. Simmer until Giovanni is able to get there.

Per serving: 494 calories, 18 g protein, 8 g fat (1 g sat), 92 g carbohydrates, 130 mg sodium, 188 mg calcium, 23 g fiber

TRICKS OF THE TRADE: Serving a gluten-free lover? Use gluten-free pasta. Duh!

Let me guess. This recipe caught your eye because you're a wild child at heart, on the lookout for a cheap thrill. Well, look no further, for I am the beacon to all things cheap and all things thrilling, starting with this soup. I've chosen ingredients that are remarkably inexpensive. In fact, I concocted this soup when my cupboards were bare and all that I had were a few bulk staples. From one wild child to another, trust me, your taste buds will go berserk for this creamy blend of wild rice and yellow split peas, which are given a gigantic boost of flavor with a generous helping of jalapeño chiles and a pleasing blend of herbs and spices.

wild child CHOWDER

2½ cups **water**

2 cups **finely chopped onions**

¼ cup **minced jalapeño chiles**

1½ tablespoons **minced garlic**

4 cups **salt-free vegetable broth**

1¼ cups **fresh or frozen corn kernels**

1¼ cups **peeled and diced potatoes**

¾ cup **wild rice blend** (see Tricks of the Trade)

¾ cup **dried yellow split peas,** rinsed and drained

2 teaspoons **dried oregano**

1 teaspoon **ground cumin**

Salt

Freshly ground **black pepper**

¼ cup **hempseeds,** for garnish

Heed the call of the wild. Heat ½ cup of the water in a large soup pot over medium-high heat. Add the onions and cook, stirring occasionally, until beginning to soften, about 3 minutes. Add the chiles and garlic and cook, stirring occasionally, until soft, about 2 minutes.

Add the broth, the remaining 2 cups of the water, and the corn, potatoes, wild rice blend, and split peas. Stir to combine. Increase the heat to high and bring to a boil. Decrease the heat to medium, stir in the oregano and cumin, cover, and cook until the split peas are very tender, about 40 minutes. While the chowder cooks, see if you can sow some wild oats.

Season with salt and pepper to taste. Simmer until ready to serve. Garnish each serving with a sprinkling of the hempseeds, and let the wild child out to play.

Per serving: 288 calories, 12 g protein, 4 g fat (1 g sat), 57 g carbohydrates, 42 mg sodium, 60 mg calcium, 10 g fiber

TRICKS OF THE TRADE: In case you didn't know, a wild rice blend is a packaged blend of grains, often including wild rice, brown rice, and sweet brown rice—a sort of triple threat, just like me. (Not only am I a beacon for cheap thrills, but I'm also a messenger of peace and a total badass on the badminton court.)

Heaven is here on earth, as you will soon discover once you take a bite of my out-of-this-world red lentil curry stew. Sumptuous is the word. Transcendent is the effect. Dig in and take flight!

COSMIC CURRY *stew*

1 teaspoon **curry powder**

¼ teaspoon **ground cardamom**

¼ teaspoon **ground cinnamon**

¼ teaspoon **ground dry mustard**

⅛ teaspoon **ground allspice**

⅛ teaspoon **ground turmeric**

2 cups **water**

1¼ cups **chopped onions**

1 tablespoon **minced garlic**

¾ cup **dried red lentils**

1 cup **peeled and cubed yellow potatoes**

¾ cup **full-fat coconut milk**

¾ teaspoon **salt**

Freshly ground **black pepper**

Ground control to Major Tom, put your helmet on in preparation for making this dish. (My helmet, of course, is adorned with fuschia gemstones.) Combine the curry powder, cardamom, cinnamon, dry mustard, allspice, and turmeric in a small bowl.

Heat ¼ cup of the water in a large saucepan over medium-high heat. Add the onions and garlic and cook, stirring occasionally, until softened, about 5 minutes.

Add the spice mixture and cook, stirring constantly, for 1 minute.

Add the lentils, potatoes, and the remaining 1¾ cups of the water. Stir and bring to a boil over high heat. Decrease the heat to medium-low, cover, and simmer until the lentils are very tender, 15 to 20 minutes. Commencing countdown, engines on.

Add the coconut milk and salt. Decrease the heat to low. Stir and simmer until heated through, about 5 minutes. Season with pepper to taste. Lift off!

Per serving: 193 calories, 7 g protein, 8 g fat (8 g sat), 30 g carbohydrates, 446 mg sodium, 37 mg calcium, 9 g fiber

Longing for a trip down memory lane? Aching for one of those gooey grilled cheese sandwiches that your nana used to make for you? Those flavors, textures, and fond memories can all be found here. This sandwich is a tease because it tastes like grilled cheese, but it's not. I've replaced the cheese with my cashew-based Cheeky Spread. Now if you think I'm a tease, guess again. I deliver, baby! Take a bite of this cheeky sandwich and let your nostalgia reign supreme.

what-a-tease SANDWICH

¼ cup **Cheeky Spread** (page 122)

4 slices **multigrain sandwich bread**

2 tablespoons **vegan buttery spread**

Spread 2 tablespoons of the Cheeky Spread on one slice of the bread and cover with another slice to make a cheeky sandwich. Repeat with the remaining Cheeky Spread and other bread slices.

Melt 1 tablespoon of the vegan buttery spread in a large skillet over medium heat. (Ahh, vegan buttery spread, the harbinger of nostalgia.)

Cook the sandwiches on one side until golden brown, about 3 minutes. Flip and cook on the other side until golden brown, about 3 minutes. Cut on a diagonal for the classic triangular shape. Take a bite, and it's 1985 all over again.

Per sandwich: 264 calories, 6 g protein, 17 g fat (4 g sat), 23 g carbohydrates, 589 mg sodium, 83 mg calcium, 4 g fiber

I bet you didn't know that when I'm not doing fan kicks and singing musical licks, I'm meditating on our eternal oneness. It's true. I'm a yogini at heart, and the idea for this simple sandwich was inspired by this little practice of mine, which has its origins in India. Accompanying the hearty cooked tempeh are two tantalizing

baba's TEMPEH SANDWICH

1 (8-ounce) **package tempeh**

1 tablespoon **canola oil**

½ cup **water**

1½ tablespoons **reduced-sodium soy sauce or Coconut Aminos**

1½ tablespoons **freshly squeezed lemon juice**

4 slices **multigrain bread**

6 tablespoons **Shakti Spread** (page 123)

6 tablespoons **Cha-Cha-Cha Chutney** (page 126)

1 cup **alfalfa or other sprouts**

Namaste, oh sequined one. Slice the tempeh in half crosswise, and then cut each piece in half horizontally to create four thin pieces.

Heat the oil in a medium skillet over medium heat. Add the tempeh and cook until lightly browned, about 3 minutes. Carefully flip and cook until the other side is lightly browned, 2 to 3 minutes. Add the water, soy sauce, and lemon juice. Decrease the heat to medium-low, cover, and cook until most of the liquid has evaporated, about 10 minutes. Uncover and cook until all the liquid has evaporated, about 3 minutes longer. Transfer to a plate and let cool. Downward dog while you wait.

Now that you're all stretched out, assemble the sandwiches. Spread 3 tablespoons of Shakti Spread on one slice of the bread. On another slice, spread 3 tablespoons of Cha-Cha-Cha Chutney. (Simultaneous cha-cha dance steps are recommended, but should only be attempted if you feel confident executing Latin dance steps while wielding a knife.)

Arrange two of the tempeh slices over the Shakti spread. Put half the sprouts over the tempeh and cover with the other slice of bread, chutney-side down. Repeat with the remaining bread and tempeh until you have two sandwiches to take you and another dear soul on a tantric trip to taste-bud heaven.

Per sandwich: 656 calories, 37 g protein, 25 g fat (4 g sat), 74 g carbohydrates, 1,117 mg sodium, 254 mg calcium, 18 g fiber

TRICKS OF THE TRADE: This cooked tempeh can be used for more than just sandwiches. Chop up the cooked tempeh and add it to Flaming Stir Fry (page 106), Mondo Salade (page 60), or Peanut-Pea Pasta (page 116). You could also crumble it and use as the veggie burger crumbles in Lip-Smackin' Lasagna (page 104).

sandwich spreads—one a curried sunflower seed and red lentil mash-up and the other a sweet-and-spicy mango chutney. I hope this sacred sandwich inspires you to discover the bliss of freedom within your very own self! *Om shanti,* my peeps.

In a flaming hurry?

If you don't have time to make Shakti Spread or Cha-Cha-Cha Chutney, you can easily replace these homemade spreads. Try using a prepared vegan mayonnaise on one slice of bread and Dijon mustard on the other. Your sandwich won't have an Indian flair, but it will be a whole different kind of scrumptious—the fast and easy kind. Just like me.

Are you ready to rumble? If so, then make these ginger-infused sloppy Joes for your next Super Bowl party. Invite all the hot jocks on your block and have them bring the chips, the dips, and the testosterone. I have my outfit all picked out (see photo, page 131). Now I just have to learn a thing or two about baseball. I want to be able to talk about the big game with the guys as I'm feeding their beefcake appetites from my very own kitchen. (I'm going to look so cute wearing just a belted jersey and a pair of red pumps!) I have a feeling this Asian-inspired hungry-man chow is going to hit a home run, and with luck, by the end of the night, so will I.

SLOPPY *gingers*

1 tablespoon **toasted sesame oil**

1 cup **chopped red onions**

½ cup **sliced scallions**

2 tablespoons **diced celery**

1 tablespoon **minced garlic**

1 tablespoon **peeled and minced fresh ginger**

1 pound **tempeh, crumbled**

2 tablespoons **reduced-sodium soy sauce or Coconut Aminos**

1 (15-ounce) can **salt-free diced tomatoes, drained**

½ cup **ketchup**

1 tablespoon **freshly squeezed lime juice**

Salt

Freshly ground **black pepper**

10 **sandwich buns, or** 20 slices **sandwich bread**

Let's play ball. Heat the oil in a large skillet over medium-high heat. Add the onions, scallions, celery, garlic, and ginger. Cook, stirring frequently, until softened, about 5 minutes.

Add the tempeh and soy sauce and cook, stirring occasionally, until the tempeh is lightly browned, 3 to 5 minutes. (While we wait for that to cook, I'm going to give us a topic for discussion: Jockstraps. Who was the brilliant homo who invented these and where can I pay homage to him?)

Add the tomatoes, ketchup, and lime juice. Stir until well combined and decrease the heat to medium. Cook, stirring occasionally, until warmed through, about 5 minutes. Season with salt and pepper to taste.

Fill each sandwich bun with about ½ cup of the tempeh mixture.

Once all of your jockular guests have plated up and planted themselves on the sofa in front of the TV, wedge yourself in between them. Get cozy. Now that's my idea of a huddle. The big game suddenly got a lot more interesting. Score for Ginger!

Per sandwich: 298 calories, 16 g protein, 8 g fat (2 g sat), 41 g carbohydrates, 691 mg sodium, 107 mg calcium, 3 g fiber

You can get fresh with me anytime, buster, but if you really want to melt my vegan buttery spread, make me lunch. Nothing impresses me more than a self-proclaimed carnivore who goes the extra mile to make a vegan dish for me. I'll melt in your arms! That said, I can't possibly join each and every one of you for lunch in your respective corners of the globe. You'll have to find another vegan chick to impress with a chickpea wrap. These deliciously fresh wraps are no-brainers to prepare, perfect for a dimwitted hunk like yourself. Before you know it, you'll be pitching the woo to some other pink-haired vixen who's caught your eye.

chickpea WRAP-IN-A-SNAP

1 (15-ounce) can **salt-free chickpeas, rinsed and drained**

½ cup **vegan mayonnaise**

½ cup **seedless green grapes, halved**

⅓ cup **sliced scallion greens**

⅓ cup **diced green bell pepper**

¼ cup **minced fresh parsley**

3 tablespoons **diced celery**

1 tablespoon **chopped fresh dill, or 1 teaspoon dried dill weed**

1 tablespoon **freshly squeezed lemon juice**

Freshly ground **black pepper**

4 **whole-grain tortilla wraps**

4 cups **spinach**

Easy chickpeas-y. One, two, three-sy. Put the chickpeas, vegan mayonnaise, grapes, scallion greens, bell pepper, parsley, celery, dill, and lemon juice in a medium bowl. Stir until well combined. Season with pepper to taste. Looky there—you've made chickpea salad.

Put a tortilla on a plate. Cover the center of the tortilla with 1 cup of the spinach. Spoon one-quarter of the chickpea salad over the spinach. Wrap the sides of the tortilla around the filling and secure the wrap closed with a toothpick. Repeat with the remaining tortillas and chickpea salad to make four wraps-in-a-snap.

Serve with a hunky smile, and remind your lunch date that there's a toothpick in the wrap that she'll need to remove *before* eating. Nothing puts a damper on a date more than a trip to the emergency room. Though the infamous blender incident of 2005 proved to be a bonding moment for me and the boyfriend who rushed me to the emergency room. We stayed together for nearly two weeks, a Mistress Ginger relationship record.

Per wrap: 432 calories, 12 g protein, 22 g fat (1 g sat), 45 g carbohydrates, 417 mg sodium, 103 mg calcium, 9 g fiber

It's time to get chichi, folks. I know you think I just cavort in the junkyard all day long, but I'm just as likely to be found at a ritzy Parisian café with a cosmopolitan corporate crackerjack. After he gives me a sparkling token of his esteem in a velveteen box, we make a toast to our torrid liaison, and then chow down on a couple of these roasted vegetable sandwiches. You too can feel Parisian for about five seconds when you

CHICHI *panini*

1 **eggplant**

1 **red bell pepper**

1 tablespoon **extra-virgin olive oil**, plus more for oiling the baking sheet

Salt

Freshly ground **black pepper**

1 (20-inch) **French baguette**

1½ cups **Par-tay Pâté** (page 124)

1 cup **baby arugula**

When he arrives at your place, start making the panini. Preheat the oven to 350 degrees F, and try this line on your lover: *"Fait-il chaud ici, ou c'est juste vous?"* (Is it hot in here, or is it just you?)

Lightly oil a baking sheet.

Slice the eggplant lengthwise into about six slices, each ¼ inch thick. Slice the bell pepper lengthwise into about nine slices, each about 1 inch wide. Toss the eggplant and bell pepper slices with the oil in a large bowl until lightly coated.

Arrange the vegetables in a single layer on the prepared baking sheet. Lightly sprinkle with salt and pepper. Bake for 20 minutes, until somewhat tender. Now try saying, *"Embrassez-moi, je parle français."* (Kiss me, I speak French.) That's a little subtle for my taste, but you can kick it up a notch with the right body language.

Remove the pan from the oven, flip the vegetables, lightly sprinkle with salt and pepper, and return to the oven to bake for 15 to 20 minutes longer, until very tender. While the veggies cook, you might say something casual like *"Vous êtes mon soul mate. Je veux passer la reste de ma vie avec vous."* (You're my soul mate. I want to spend the rest of my life with you.)

Transfer the vegetables to a plate to cool to room temperature and get down to business. *"Connaisez-vous les contrat de mariage?"* (Do you know what a prenuptial agreement is?) If the answer is no, press on!

bite into a baguette smeared with delicate mushroom-walnut pâté and stuffed with succulent roasted veggies. A few French phrases are the only other things you'll need to drive your lover wild with desire. Let's start with something reserved: *"Voulez-vous coucher avec moi, ce soir?"*

Cut the round ends off the baguette, then cut the baguette crosswise into three pieces. Slice each piece in half horizontally. To assemble a panini, spread ¼ cup of the pâté on two slices of the bread. Arrange ⅓ cup arugula, two eggplant slices, and three bell pepper slices on one slice of bread and cover with the other slice. Repeat to make two more sandwiches.

As the evening progresses, you might find a use for a couple of other phrases: *"Voulez-vous danser avec moi? Que diriez-vous le mambo horizontale?"* (Would you like to dance with me? How about the horizontal mambo?) and *"C'etait formidable! Pourriez-vous defaire les attaches, s'il vous plait?"* (That was amazing. Would you please untie me now?)

Mmm, that *was* amazing.

Per sandwich: 582 calories, 17 g protein, 30 g fat (5 g sat), 67 g carbohydrates, 661 mg sodium, 62 mg calcium, 11 g fiber

The time has come for that snooty-tooty tea party that you always dreamed of hosting, and how could you think of leaving cucumber sandwiches off the menu? These classic sandwiches would not be complete without my signature Coconutty Cream Cheese (page 133), which you'll need to prepare in advance. If you've never hosted a tea party, take these words of wisdom from the Mistress Ginger School of Charm: wear something lacy, something bright, something sequined, something tight. And get those pinkies up!

FANCY CUCUMBER *sandwiches*

1 cucumber, peeled and thinly sliced

¼ cup thinly sliced scallion greens

1 teaspoon freshly squeezed lemon juice

2 teaspoons fresh dill, or ½ teaspoon dried dill weed

Pinch salt

¾ cup Coconutty Cream Cheese (page 133)

8 slices white or multigrain sandwich bread

Listen up, ladies. (I'm speaking to *all* of you, especially those of you sporting the lumberjack look.) Toss the cucumber, scallion greens, lemon juice, dill, and salt in a medium bowl.

Spread 1½ tablespoons of the Coconutty Cream Cheese on each slice of the bread.

On one of the bread slices, arrange one-quarter of the cucumber slices over the cream cheese and cover with another slice of bread, spread-side down. Repeat with the remaining bread slices to create four sandwiches.

If you want to get really fancy, trim the crusts off the bread. Slice each sandwich on both diagonals, creating sixteen small triangular sandwiches. Serve with a sashay and a shante for old times' sake, and feel like the girlie girl you were born to be, combat boots and all.

Per 2 sandwiches: 140 calories, 5 g protein, 4 g fat (3 g sat), 20 g carbohydrates, 74 mg sodium, 45 mg calcium, 1 g fiber

THE DELISH
MAIN DISH

This recipe is essentially a butt-naked template for a dish that can be dressed up in countless ways to suit your cravings. To fully appreciate the value of this template, imagine that you're at home expecting a dinner date but you've forgotten which one of your numerous lovers you've scheduled for tonight. Is it Junichi from Japan, Indrajit from India, or Fabrice from France? Not to fear. Just get this dish nearly

in-the-buff BEANS AND GREENS

2 tablespoons **extra-virgin olive oil**

1½ cups **chopped onions**

1 (15-ounce) **can salt-free beans** (any kind), **rinsed and drained**

4 cups **chopped greens, lightly packed**

Let's get naked. Heat the oil in a large skillet over medium-high heat. Add the onions and cook, stirring occasionally, until softened, about 5 minutes. Stir in the beans and cook for 3 minutes. Stir in the greens and cook until tender, 3 to 5 minutes. Remove from the heat, season to taste (see the variations that follow), and put your clothes back on! I wasn't being literal, for crying out loud.

Per serving: 427 calories, 18 g protein, 15 g fat (2 g sat), 61 g carbohydrates, 84 mg sodium, 321 mg calcium, 16 g fiber

TRICKS OF THE TRADE: Use whatever salt-free canned beans and fresh greens you have on hand, modify the proportions as you like, adding more or less of the beans or greens to suit your appetite, and adjust the seasonings to taste. It's high time that you started thinking of your kitchen as your own personal playground. By that, I mean that you should playfully experiment with seasoning your food, not that you should treat your butcher block like a jungle gym. Though, that's also an option.

VARIATIONS: Let's play dress-up! Approach In-the-Buff Beans and Greens in the same way that I approach my wardrobe. Let your imagination run wild. Stop at nothing to thrill those who might take a bite (and join you on your makeshift jungle gym).

done, and once he arrives you can throw in the seasonings that correspond to the country of his origin. He'll feel like he's back home again, especially when he falls into your ever-lovin' embrace. Serve this dish over a bed of leftover Gorgeous Grains (page 72) for a sensational meal in the blink of a bedroom eye.

ASIAN ADUKI BEANS AND CABBAGE: Use aduki beans for the beans and cabbage for the greens. Season with 2 teaspoons of reduced-sodium soy sauce or Coconut Aminos and 2 teaspoons of ume plum vinegar. Junichi will absolutely love it!

FRENCH LENTILS AND SPINACH: Use French lentils for the beans and spinach for the greens. Season with 1 tablespoon of freshly squeezed lemon juice, ½ teaspoon of dried tarragon, and salt and freshly ground black pepper to taste. You'll have Fabrice eating out of your hand, which could get very messy, so I recommend laying down a drop cloth before he arrives.

INDIAN CHICKPEAS AND CHARD: Use chickpeas for the beans and chard for the greens. Season with ½ teaspoon of curry powder, ⅛ teaspoon of ground ginger, ⅛ teaspoon of garlic powder, and salt to taste. Indrajit will be enthralled!

Calling all eligible bachelors with a villa in Tuscany. I'm single, willing to relocate, and serious about being a part of your Mediterranean paradise. I would say that I enjoy long walks on the beach, but not in these six-inch heels! And the truth is, I don't go anywhere without my heels. On the plus side, I'm into extra-virgin olive oil, and I've been working on my Italian. Though I can't think of any Italian words right now, I am prepared to make a dish for you that features the flavors of your homeland. *Mamma mia!* Hey, there's some Italian for you. And come to think of it, I know one other Italian word: *Mangia! Mangia!*

MEDITERRANEAN *mélange*

QUINOA-MILLET PILAF

½ cup **quinoa**

¼ cup **millet**

1½ cups **water**

Salt

2 teaspoons **extra-virgin olive oil**

1 tablespoon **minced fresh parsley**

Freshly ground **black pepper**

WHITE BEANS AND KALE

1½ tablespoons **extra-virgin olive oil**

½ cup **chopped red onion**

1 tablespoon **minced garlic**

1 (15-ounce) can **salt-free great Northern beans, rinsed and drained**

5 cups **coarsely chopped kale, lightly packed**

½ cup **kalamata olives, rinsed and sliced**

⅓ cup **chopped oil-packed sun-dried tomatoes**

2 teaspoons **red wine vinegar**

1 teaspoon **dried oregano**

Salt

Freshly ground **black pepper**

Step one in the universal quest for an Italian stallion is to prepare a light quinoa-millet pilaf. Put the quinoa, millet, water, and a pinch of salt in a medium saucepan and bring to a boil over high heat. Decrease the heat to medium-low, add the 2 teaspoons of oil, cover, and simmer until the grains are cooked and all the water is absorbed, about 15 minutes. Let sit covered for 5 minutes. Stir in the parsley and season with salt and pepper to taste.

While the pilaf cooks, pray to Mount Vesuvias that your loverboy will materialize within the next 15 minutes, and then prepare the white beans and kale. Heat the 1½ tablespoons of oil in a large skillet over medium-high heat. Add the onion and cook, stirring occasionally, until softened, about 5 minutes. Add the garlic and cook, stirring constantly, until fragrant, 1 minute. Add the beans and cook, stirring occasionally, until warmed through, about 3 minutes. Add the kale and cook, stirring occasionally, until tender, about 5 minutes. After all that stirring, you'll probably be worked up into a manic frenzy. That's good. Now you understand how I feel most of the time. Channel that energy into conjuring your bella beloved.

Remove from the heat and stir in the olives, tomatoes, vinegar, and oregano. Season with salt and pepper to taste, and check to see if your Italian heartthrob is waiting for you on the front doorstep. What? He's not there? Just the crickets chirping? I don't understand. It always works for me.

For each serving, put half the kale mixture over a mound of pilaf, and then resort to plan B. Build a cardboard cutout of a guy, call him Guido, and sit him down at the dining room table across from you. Light some candles, feast on your Mediterranean Mélange, and try your best to get romantic until the real thing comes along, or until you get a paper cut, whichever comes first.

Per serving: 455 calories, 15 g protein, 18 g fat (3 g sat), 59 g carbohydrates, 281 mg sodium, 207 mg calcium, 11 g fiber

A few years ago, I invited a young suitor over to my house for a little supper. He happened to be one of those self-proclaimed carnivores and a total tofu naysayer. Double whammy! Well, if nothing else, I was determined to change his mind about soybean curd. This dish did the trick, as it always does. Sure, I served it to him wearing just an apron, but I think what sealed the deal was this sweet yet savory, hearty yet healthy, squash-tofu combo served over a pile of Gorgeous Grains (page 72). Let's just say that all the scantily clad dishes served that night were devoured by morning.

scantily-clad SQUASH AND TOFU

2 tablespoons **extra-virgin olive oil**

3½ cups **peeled and cubed acorn squash**

½ cup **chopped onion**

1 pound **extra-firm tofu, cubed**

¾ teaspoon **salt**

½ teaspoon **freshly ground black pepper**

2 teaspoons **reduced-sodium soy sauce or Coconut Aminos**

½ cup **chopped scallions**

Put on your apron over your birthday suit. Heat the oil in a large saucepan over medium-high heat.

Add the squash and onion and cook, stirring frequently, until the squash is almost tender, about 10 minutes. Add the tofu, salt, and pepper and cook, stirring almost constantly, until the tofu starts to brown, about 5 minutes. The squash should become very tender and begin to disintegrate, smearing its deliciousness all over the tofu.

Stir in the soy sauce and scallions and cook, stirring frequently, until the scallions are tender but still bright green, about 2 minutes.

Remove from the heat, cover, and let sit for 5 minutes so the flavors can get to know one another. Serve this scantily clad combo while wearing just three things: an apron, a pair of bobby socks, and a great big smile.

Per serving: 338 calories, 19 g protein, 17 g fat (3 g sat), 32 g carbohydrates, 593 mg sodium, 218 mg calcium, 9 g fiber

I adore everything about Brazil, from the bright, bold colors to the sweet, sexy samba to the tall, dark, and handsome locals. In fact, one of those strapping locals taught me how to make the Brazilian black beans that are the centerpiece of this vibrant platter. Have I whet your appetite yet? These sexy beans are adorned with a colorful array of fresh vegetables, all of which can be prepared within minutes, leaving more time for . . . samba!

brazilian RAINBOW PLATTER

2 tablespoons **minced garlic**

1 teaspoon **salt**

2 tablespoons **extra-virgin olive oil**

2 (15-ounce) cans **salt-free black beans, rinsed and drained**

2 cups **peeled and chopped yams or carrots**

4 cups **chopped kale or collard greens, lightly packed**

4 cups **cooked brown rice**

2 **tomatoes, each cut into about 8 wedges**

1 **ripe avocado, sliced**

Freshly squeezed **lemon juice**

Salt

Freshly ground **black pepper**

First, give that garlic the ol' bump and grind! That's right, grind the garlic and salt in a mortar with pestle (or in a food processor) until a paste forms and the juicy goodness of the garlic is set free.

Heat the oil in a medium saucepan over medium-high heat, about 1 minute. Add the garlic paste and cook, stirring constantly, for 1 minute. Add the beans and decrease the heat to medium. Cook, stirring occasionally, until the beans are heated through, about 5 minutes.

If you're teaching your lover to make this dish, this is when you stand behind him, holding his hand in yours and guiding him to press some of the beans up against the side of the saucepan with the spoon until about half are mashed and half are still somewhat formed. (We're taking "spooning" to the next level here. Please *do* try this at home.)

Put about 1 inch of water in a large saucepan with a vegetable steamer. Bring to a boil. Add the yams, cover, and steam until nearly tender, about 5 minutes. Put the kale over the yams, cover, and steam until the yams and kale are tender, about 2 minutes. (Still spooning by the stove? A little nibble on the earlobe works wonders here.)

For each serving, put 1 cup of rice on a plate or in a shallow bowl. Put one-quarter of the beans over the rice. Arrange one-quarter of the vegetables and tomato wedges around the beans. Garnish with a few avocado slices. Season with lemon juice, salt, and pepper to taste. Serve this magnificent feast to your tall, dark, and handsome dreamboat, and say, "*Bom apetite!*"

Per serving: 633 calories, 20 g protein, 16 g fat (2 g sat), 105 g carbohydrates, 652 mg sodium, 223 mg calcium, 199 g fiber

Is that a tortelloni in your pocket, or are you just happy to see me? What's a tortelloni? It's an Italian dumpling, like tortellini but a bit larger. You're not going to find too many of them of the vegan variety. Here, however, the tortelloni has been veganized using Nottaricotta (page 132) as the filling. Toss with Presto Pesto (page 129), Alfredo's Sauce (page 128), or one of your other favorite pasta sauces for a dazzling dish that no bodacious body can resist. So maybe now you can answer me: Is that a tortelloni in your pocket, or what?

bodacious TORTELLONI

2 tablespoons **Ener-G Egg Replacer**

1 cup **water**

2 teaspoons **extra-virgin olive oil**

2 cups **unbleached all-purpose flour**, plus more for rolling the dough

½ teaspoon **salt**

1¼ cups **Nottaricotta** (page 132)

This ain't no phony tortelloni. If you want the real thing, you're going to have to begin by making some dough. Combine the egg replacer with ½ cup of the water in a food processor and process until frothy, about 3 minutes. Add the oil and process for 30 seconds longer.

Put the flour and salt in a large bowl. Whisk until well combined. Add the egg replacer mixture and beat with an electric mixer until crumbly. Add the additional water, 1 tablespoon at a time, and mix until a dough begins to form. Add just enough water so that the dough sticks together.

With your hands, form the dough into two compact balls, dust with flour, wrap tightly in plastic wrap, and chill for at least 30 minutes. This is a good time to prepare the Nottaricotta. Or, if that's already done, you can use this time to have an out-of-body experience. I hear that Costa Rica is really lovely this time of year.

Once the dough is chilled, dust a countertop with flour. Roll one of the dough balls into a ⅛-inch-thick circle, adding flour to keep the dough from becoming sticky. Cut the rolled dough into 2½-inch squares.

Now pay attention (and try not to get distracted by that scandalous picture of me on page 90). To form the tortelloni, put 2 teaspoons of Nottaricotta in the center of each square. Moisten the edges of two adjoining sides of the square with a little water. Fold the other two sides over the Nottaricotta to join with the wet edges. Press the edges down to firmly "glue" the sides together to form a triangular shape. Flip so that the glued side faces up. Pick up one tortelloni and place a finger on top of the bulbous filling-side of the triangle. With your other hand, wrap the corners of the dough around your finger to meet one another. Moisten the end of one corner and adjoin it to the other corner. Press firmly to "glue" the corners together. And there you have it—one tortelloni. Am I making any sense? Have I lost you completely?

If you're still here and haven't pulled out all your hair (or become, shall we say, preoccupied with that picture of me on page 87), repeat with the remainder of the dough squares and with the other ball of dough.

When all 30 tortelloni have been rolled, bring a large pot of lightly salted water to a boil. Add half of the tortelloni to the pot of boiling water. Be gentle with them. They're not made of wrought iron. Boil until fully cooked, tender but somewhat firm, about 7 minutes. Stir very gently just to be sure the tortelloni aren't sticking to the bottom of the pot; they will float to the top of the water when done.

Scoop them out of the water with a slotted spoon and transfer to a colander. Add the other half of the tortelloni to the pot, cook in the same way, and transfer to the colander when done. Whatever you do, don't put the tortelloni in your pocket for safekeeping. I did that once, and it led to a lot of confusion for my date.

He asked, "Is that a tortelloni in your pocket, or what?"

"A tortelloni," I said, removing the squashed dumpling from my pocket.

He was relieved, but my dry cleaner was none too thrilled.

Per serving: 425 calories, 18 g protein, 18 g fat (0.3 g sat), 48 g carbohydrates, 365 mg sodium, 185 mg calcium, 2 g fiber

TOTALLY TORTELLINI: If you're not such a size queen and you'd be happy with a smaller version of tortelloni, commonly known as tortellini, cut the dough into 2-inch squares and fill with just 1 teaspoon of Nottaricotta.

TRICKS OF THE TRADE: If you're making Presto Pesto (page 129) or Alfredo's Sauce (page 128) for the tortelloni, either recipe will provide just the right amount of sauce to cover about 30 tortelloni. Isn't that convenient?

Here we have layers upon layers of the saucy and the sublime. You think I'm talking about myself again, but I'm not! True, I do have many layers compared to your typical vegan yogi showgirl with pink hair. However, in this case, I'm speaking of the saucy and sublime layers in my vegan lasagna, one of the few recipes in this book

LIP-SMACKIN' *lasagna*

1 (16-ounce) box **lasagna noodles**

2 tablespoons **olive oil**

⅓ cup **chopped onion**

2 cups **coarsely chopped crimini mushrooms** (about ½-inch pieces)

¼ cup **minced garlic**

2 (28-ounce) cans **salt-free crushed tomatoes**

1½ teaspoons **dried basil**

½ teaspoon **dried thyme**

½ teaspoon **dried oregano**

½ teaspoon **salt**

1 (12-ounce) package **veggie protein crumbles**, prepared according to package directions

4½ cups **Nottaricotta** (page 132)

1 (8-ounce) package **shredded nondairy mozzarella cheese**

Wannabe lip-smackers, listen up. Preheat the oven to 350 degrees F. Cook and drain the noodles according to the package directions. *Capiche?*

Prepare the sauce while the pasta is cooking. Heat the oil in a large saucepan over medium-high heat. Add the onion and cook, stirring frequently, until softened, about 3 minutes. Add the mushrooms and cook, stirring frequently, until softened, 5 to 7 minutes. Add the garlic and cook, stirring occasionally, for 1 to 2 minutes. Stir in the tomatoes, basil, thyme, oregano, and salt and simmer for 5 minutes. Put 1 cup of the sauce in a measuring cup or small bowl and set aside. Stir the veggie protein crumbles into the remaining sauce. Decrease the heat to medium-low and simmer for at least 15 minutes.

If you think you're going to run to the TV right now to catch a bit of your favorite soap opera, guess again. While the sauce simmers, prepare a double batch of Nottaricotta (page 132).

Now we layer the saucy and the sublime. Cover the bottom of a 13 x 9 inch baking dish with ½ cup of the reserved sauce (the thin sauce without the veggie protein crumbles). Arrange 4 lasagna noodles lengthwise with overlapping edges to create a layer that covers the bottom of the baking dish. Using a rubber spatula, smear half the Nottaricotta over the noodles. Drizzle about 1½ cups of the sauce with the veggie protein crumbles over the Nottaricotta. Sprinkle one-quarter of the nondairy cheese over the sauce. Repeat this process, layering 4 lasagna noodles, the remaining Nottaricotta, 1½ cups of the sauce with the veggie protein crumbles, and one-quarter of the nondairy cheese. Add a final layer of lasagna noodles and cover with the remaining ½ cup of the reserved sauce. Sprinkle with the remaining nondairy cheese. I'm keeping you busy, aren't I?

that makes use of some of those newfangled vegan foods on the market: dairy-free cheese, egg-free mayo, and veggie protein crumbles. These somewhat processed products are a fun treat every now and then, as they enable us to make our old favorites without much fuss, getting us to the actual lip-smackin' that much sooner.

Cover with aluminum foil. Put the baking dish in the center of the oven and put a baking sheet on the rack below to catch any liquid that might boil over as the lasagna cooks. Bake for 30 minutes. All right, now you can take a break to watch your stories. That, or use the time to prepare a couple of side dishes to complement this tour de force of an entrée.

Remove the foil and bake for 10 minutes longer, until the nondairy cheese on the top has melted. Remove from the oven and let sit for about 10 minutes. Spoon the remaining sauce around each individual serving. Take a bite and become immersed in the layers of saucy and sublime, the young and the restless, the bold and the beautiful, the trashy and the trifling.

Per serving: 507 calories, 24 g protein, 27 g fat (3 g sat), 42 g carbohydrates, 445 mg sodium, 208 mg calcium, 5 g fiber

A stir-fry might sound boring to you, and honestly it sometimes sounds boring to me. But then I make it, and even I, flaming showgirl supreme, am thoroughly satisfied by the stir-fry experience. Oh, to feast on a plate of vibrant vegetables served over Gorgeous Grains (page 72), my body says "yes!" This dish is perfect

flaming STIR-FRY

2 tablespoons plus 2 teaspoons **reduced-sodium soy sauce or Coconut Aminos**

¼ teaspoon **ground ginger**

¼ teaspoon **garlic powder**

¼ teaspoon **onion powder**

2 tablespoons **coconut oil**

1 pound **extra-firm tofu, cubed**

1 large **onion, cut in half and sliced into ¼-inch-thick half-moons**

2 **carrots, peeled and cut diagonally into ¼-inch-thick slices**

1 cup **thinly sliced green cabbage**

1 cup **thinly sliced red cabbage**

1 tablespoon **minced garlic**

1 tablespoon **peeled and minced fresh ginger**

1½ cups **small broccoli florets**

4 cups **chopped kale or collard greens**

3 cups **Gorgeous Grains** (page 72)

Word to the flaming wise: prepare all your vegetables first. Get all that chopping, slicing, and mincing out of the way before you start cooking.

Mix 2 teaspoons of the soy sauce and the ground ginger, garlic powder, and onion powder in a medium bowl.

Heat the oil in a large skillet or wok over medium-high heat. Add the tofu and cook, stirring occasionally, until browned on all sides, 5 to 7 minutes. Once the tofu is browned, add it to the soy sauce mixture in the bowl. Toss to coat the tofu and set aside.

Now you can go to town like the stir-fry diva that you are. Add the onion and carrots to the skillet or wok and cook, stirring frequently, until beginning to soften, about 5 minutes. Add the green and red cabbage and cook, stirring frequently, until beginning to soften, about 3 minutes. Add the garlic and fresh ginger and cook until fragrant, stirring frequently, about 2 minutes. Add the broccoli and cook until tender-crisp, stirring occasionally, about 3 minutes. Add the kale and cook until tender, stirring occasionally, about 2 minutes.

When all the vegetables are tender but still bright and colorful, add the remaining 2 tablespoons of soy sauce and stir to evenly distribute. Fold the tofu into the stir-fry and cook until heated through, about 2 minutes.

For each serving, put one-quarter of the stir-fried veggies over a mound of Gorgeous Grains. Present your flaming stir-fry with as much flamboyance as you can muster. I have a feeling that, as far as flamboyance goes, you don't need coaching. In fact, I could probably learn a thing or two from you, ya big ol' flamer.

Per serving: 347 calories, 24 g protein, 19 g fat (9 g sat), 24 g carbohydrates, 605 mg sodium, 291 mg calcium, 5 g fiber
Note: Nutritional analysis does not include grains.

when you're in a flaming hurry, and it can be easily altered to include whatever veggies you happen to have on hand. While the list of ingredients may appear long, this recipe couldn't be simpler. No more excuses, you flamer, you. Have a stir-fry and like it. Your Mistress has spoken.

TRICKS OF THE TRADE: As a general rule when making a stir-fry, begin by cooking the denser vegetables first. When they begin to soften, add the next batch of somewhat lighter veggies. As with any stir-fry, the heat should be medium high, and the stirring should be rather constant. The dish should cook quickly so that the vegetables are somewhat tender but still bright with color and not at all mushy. Your Mistress loves to dole out rules, but as you and I both know, rules are made to be broken (just take a look at the photo on page 21 to see what I mean).

VARIATIONS

- Use whatever vegetables you have on hand. Other wonderful add-ins include bok choy, Chinese cabbage, eggplant, mushrooms, red onion, and scallions. It's another opportunity for playtime in your kitchen. Explore, experiment, and exorcise those humdrum demons.
- Omit the tofu or replace it with the cooked tempeh (cubed) from Baba's Tempeh Sandwich (page 86) or with a 15-ounce can of salt-free beans. Chickpeas would be splendid. Just add the beans around the same time that you add the garlic and fresh ginger, giving them enough time to warm through and absorb the flavors around them.
- For an added boost of vitality, throw in a handful of toasted almonds or cashews or Potent Pepitas (page 63).
- To make this dish a tad more sumptuous, drizzle individual servings with Hot Mess Dressing (page 121).

When I'm stirring my risotto for what seems like days, I imagine that I'm stirring my love potion, my love potion number 382. It even looks like love, thanks to the miniature edible hearts. Tender beet slices cut into the shape of Valentine hearts are guaranteed to charm the socks off your lover, quite literally! What's more, the

VALENTINE *risotto*

6 cups **salt-free vegetable broth**

½ cup **dry white wine** (optional)

3 **red beets** (about 1¼ pounds)

2 tablespoons **extra-virgin olive oil**

1 **fennel bulb, thinly sliced** (about 1 cup)

½ cup **minced shallots**

1 tablespoon **minced garlic**

½ teaspoon **ground fennel**

2 cups **arborio rice**

1½ cups **frozen shelled edamame, steamed until tender**

Salt

Freshly ground **black pepper**

¼ cup **chopped fresh chives,** for garnish

First and foremost, invoke Venus, Cupid, and any other deity of love that gets your heart racing. Then heat the broth and optional wine in a large saucepan over medium-high heat. When the broth reaches a near-boiling simmer, decrease the heat to medium-low.

To prepare the beet hearts, peel the beets and slice into ¼-inch-thick rounds. Cut each round into a heart shape by cutting a small triangle at the top of the round, then cutting away the lower sides to create a point at the bottom. You can leave the heart with an angular shape or get extra fancy and try to round the edges. (I like my hearts with a little edge to them, just like my lovers.) Add the beet parts that have been cut away from the hearts to the broth. (The broth will become red. Don't be frightened.)

Steam the beet hearts for 10 to 12 minutes, until you can easily pierce the hearts with a fork. Imagine that you're Cupid and the fork is a bow and arrow (or something silly like that). Remove the beets and set aside.

Once the broth is colored a pleasing pink, strain it through a colander into a clean medium saucepan to remove the beet pieces. (Discard those beet pieces or save them to add to a Threesome Salad, page 58.) Simmer the broth over low heat.

Heat the oil in a large skillet over medium-high heat. Add the sliced fennel and shallots and cook, stirring occasionally, until beginning to soften, about 5 minutes. Add the garlic and cook, stirring occasionally, until the fennel begins to brown, about 5 minutes. Add the ground fennel and cook, stirring constantly, for 30 seconds. Add the rice and cook, stirring constantly, for 2 minutes.

beets give the risotto a vibrant pink-red color—the color commonly associated with love (or with my hair). And if that's not enough, this dish is downright hearty (pun thoroughly intended), ensuring that you'll have plenty of energy for after-dinner activities.

Add one ladleful of beet broth to the rice. Stir until the broth has been absorbed. Continue this process, adding one ladleful of broth to the rice at a time and stirring constantly until most of the broth has been absorbed. The rice will turn pink—and pink, as you know, is my signature color.

After about a half hour of this nonsense, when the broth is nearly gone and the rice is tender and creamy but not mushy, fold in the edamame and the beet hearts. Simmer, adding additional broth if necessary, until the edamame and beets are warmed through, about 5 minutes. Season with salt and pepper to taste. Garnish individual servings with chives and serve to your valentine(s).

If somebody doesn't like your pink risotto, just blame it on the beets. If somebody doesn't like my pink hair, they can just kiss my grits.

Per serving: 564 calories, 19 g protein, 11 g fat (2 g sat), 104 g carbohydrates, 169 mg sodium, 86 mg calcium, 8 g fiber

Let's get down and dirty, folks. By that I mean let's make some jambalaya. What did you think I meant? You dirty birdie, you think you know me so well. Well, you didn't know me when I was living in New Orleans, singing in the jazz dives by night and apprenticing with a Cajun chef by day. He taught me how to worship the holy trinity. I asked, "What holy trinity?" Until then, I just thought the holy trinity was "safe, sane, and

DOWN-AND-DIRTY *jambalaya*

YIELDS 6 SERVINGS

1½ cups **long-grain brown rice**

3 cups **water**

2 **bay leaves**

Salt

3 tablespoons **extra-virgin olive oil**

½ cup **chopped onion**

½ cup **chopped celery**

½ cup **chopped green bell pepper**

3 cups **stemmed and chopped white button mushrooms**

¾ cup **seeded and chopped tomatoes**

¾ cup **chopped scallions**

2 tablespoons **minced garlic**

2 tablespoons **minced jalapeño chile**

1 tablespoon **Cajun seasoning**

1 (15-ounce) can **salt-free chickpeas, rinsed and drained**

7 ounces **kielbasa-style vegan sausages, sliced**

Freshly ground **black pepper**

¼ cup **minced fresh parsley, lightly packed**

Let's talk dirty. Combine the rice, water, bay leaves, and a pinch of salt in a large saucepan. Bring to a boil over high heat. Cover and cook until the rice is tender and all the water has been absorbed, about 45 minutes. Remove from the heat and let sit covered for 5 minutes. Remove the bay leaves, fluff the rice with a fork, and drizzle with 1 tablespoon of the oil. (Hmm, "fluff" and "drizzle." That could qualify as dirty talk, if improperly applied.)

While the rice cooks, let's take care of the holy trinity. Here's how we get holy: heat the remaining 2 tablespoons of the oil in a large soup pot over medium-high heat. Add the onion, celery, and bell pepper. Cook, stirring frequently, until softened, about 3 minutes.

Add the mushrooms, tomatoes, scallions, garlic, chile, and Cajun seasoning. Cook, stirring occasionally, until the mushrooms are tender, 5 to 7 minutes. Add the chickpeas and vegan sausage and stir to combine. Cook until the sausage is heated through, about 3 minutes. Stir in the rice and season with salt and pepper to taste. Decrease the heat to low and simmer, stirring occasionally, until the flavors have blended, about 5 minutes. Meanwhile, festoon your dining room for a Mardi Gras celebration with an indiscriminate spray of purple, green, and gold accoutrements.

consensual." But in Cajun land, the holy trinity refers to onion, celery, and bell pepper. Who knew? I've since veganized this Cajun favorite, which usually consists of a mad mix of different meats, now replaced with meaty mushrooms, chunky chickpeas, and vegan sausage. Ooh, there's another holy trinity for you to relish with glee.

Stir in the parsley and then let the festivities begin. Leading a parade of freaky dancers and gaudy floats, carry this dynamite dish out to the bedazzled dining room. And make sure a genuine N'Orleans jazz band is bringin' up the rear. (No dirty talk was intended with that last remark, I assure you).

Per serving: 404 calories, 19 g protein, 13 g fat (2 g sat), 56 g carbohydrates, 354 mg sodium, 71 mg calcium, 9 g fiber

TRICKS OF THE TRADE: While the ingredient list is on the long side, this dish is remarkably simple to prepare, especially when you consider the impressive results. What makes a dish like this even easier is prepping all the ingredients before you begin to cook. Once you begin to cook the rice, take the next 20 minutes to clean and chop the veggies so they're ready to go when you start tackling that part of the recipe. This advance preparation will save you time, and that's time that you can use to figure out how to fit that friggin' parade into your one-bedroom apartment.

I just found out that Marilyn Monroe was crowned the first Artichoke Queen in 1948. What? How did I not know this? And more importantly, why haven't I been crowned Artichoke Queen yet? I'm the queen of everything else, why not artichokes too? But I'm sure that once word gets out about my Fit-for-a-Queen Artichokes,

FIT-FOR-A-QUEEN *artichokes*

STUFFED ARTICHOKES

4 whole **artichokes**

3 tablespoons **extra-virgin olive oil**

3 cups **cubed French bread**

1 tablespoon **white balsamic vinegar**

⅓ cup **nondairy Parmesan cheese**

Salt

Freshly ground **black pepper**

1 cup **shredded nondairy mozzarella cheese**

GARLIC AÏOLI

¼ cup **vegan mayonnaise**

2 teaspoons **minced garlic**

½ teaspoon **freshly squeezed lemon juice**

First queenly duty: Put on a tiara and prep the artichokes. Cut off the artichoke stems to create flat bottoms so the artichokes can stand upright. Peel off the first two layers of leaves at the base. With scissors, remove the pointed tips from all the remaining leaves and snip 1 inch off the top. Snip, snip.

Fill a large soup pot with 4 quarts of water and bring to a boil over high heat.

Add 1 tablespoon of the oil and the artichokes and boil for 25 minutes. (Come on now! Did Marilyn ever even *boil* an artichoke?) Drain the artichokes in a colander and let cool, about 10 minutes.

While the artichokes are boiling, preheat the oven to 350 degrees F. If the kitchen gets too toasty, go outside and stand over a subway vent to cool off. (This works best if you're wearing a flare skirt, and if you live near a subway.)

To make the stuffing, put the bread on a baking sheet and bake for about 5 minutes, until the cubes are lightly toasted, crispy on the outside but soft on the inside. Remove from the oven and put in a medium bowl. (Leave the oven turned on as you will soon be baking the artichokes.)

Drizzle the vinegar and the remaining 2 tablespoons of the oil over the bread cubes and toss until moistened. Stir in the nondairy Parmesan cheese. Season with salt and pepper to taste.

To prepare the artichokes for stuffing, stand them up on their bottoms. Pick up each artichoke with tongs and use a spoon to remove the center and scrape out the fuzzy leaves while leaving the center choke and exterior leaves intact.

Fill the center cavity with the stuffing. Fan the outer leaves and stuff each leaf with a bit of stuffing. Now for the coronation. Cue fanfare. Crown each artichoke with ¼ cup of the nondairy mozzarella cheese.

I'll be hailed as the next Artichoke Queen. I knew that diamonds were a girl's best friend, but I had no idea that one might say the same for artichokes, especially when they're stuffed with breadcrumbs, smothered in vegan cheese, and dipped in garlic aïoli. Long live the queen!

Bake for 20 minutes, until the crown of nondairy mozzarella cheese has melted.

While the artichokes bake, prepare the garlic aïoli. Mix the vegan mayonnaise, garlic, and lemon juice in a small bowl. Divide the aïoli among four small dipping bowls.

Serve and eat these things like the raging queen that you are. Oh, you want to know *how* to eat these things? See Tricks of the Trade to learn how to enjoy this royal entrée to the max.

Per serving: 461 calories, 14 g protein, 27 g fat (4 g sat), 40 g carbohydrates, 748 mg sodium, 198 mg calcium, 11 g fiber

TRICKS OF THE TRADE: Eat your cooked artichokes like the queen of your childhood dreams—regally, but with your fingers. Pull off the outer leaves, one at a time, keeping your pinkies up for some majestic allure. Dip the fleshy end of each leaf in the garlic aïoli and eat the soft, fleshy part of each leaf. Continue until all the leaves have been removed. Finally, you've arrived at the heart of the artichoke. Go on, eat your heart out, and crown me Artichoke Queen!

Buddy was one of my many lovers. He was a great cook, but not vegan. Naturally he wanted to share his home cooking with me, and he soon realized that a number of his favorite dishes were already vegan or nearly so. Buddy once made me a couscous and black bean salad that I just adored. Of course, we broke up before I could get the recipe from him, so I had to guesstimate the ingredients and create my own version of this fresh summer salad. Ah, this is love. This is life. These fleeting romances are not failures. We have an experience, we learn, we grow, and ultimately each of us builds our own burrito bowl.

BUDDY'S *burrito bowl*

2 cups **water**

1⅓ cups **couscous**

2 cups **salt-free cooked or canned black beans**, rinsed and drained

¾ cup **diced red onion**

¾ cup **diced red bell pepper**

½ cup **chopped cilantro**, firmly packed

1 tablespoon **minced garlic**

1 tablespoon **minced jalapeño chile**

2 tablespoons **extra-virgin olive oil**

2 tablespoons **red wine vinegar**

2 tablespoons **freshly squeezed lime juice**, plus more as needed

Salt

Freshly ground **black pepper**

1 cup **Kickass Guacamole** (page 130; optional)

1 cup **Cheeky Sauce** (see variation, page 122; optional)

Bravely build your own burrito bowl. Start by bringing the water to a boil in a medium saucepan. Stir in the couscous, remove from the heat, cover, and let sit for 10 minutes. Uncover, fluff with a fork, and let cool to room temperature.

While the couscous cooks, combine the beans, onion, bell pepper, cilantro, garlic, chile, oil, vinegar, and lime juice in a medium bowl. Stir and let sit for at least 5 minutes to allow the flavors to mingle.

When the couscous has cooled, transfer it to a large bowl and fluff with the fork. Add the black bean mixture and stir to incorporate. Season with salt, pepper, and additional lime juice to taste. Cover and chill for at least 1 hour before serving.

If desired (and who doesn't desire?), put a dollop of Kickass Guacamole, Cheeky Sauce, or both over each serving.

Per serving: 366 calories, 13 g protein, 9 g fat (1 g sat), 55 g carbohydrates, 17 mg sodium, 112 mg calcium, 9 g fiber

GLUTEN-FREE BURRITO BOWL: Replace the couscous with 3 cups of cooked quinoa and have yourself a gluten-free fiesta.

Feeling brain-dead and ravenous? Look no further. This simple dish is nutritious, delicious, and filling. It's a party in a bowl: pasta tossed with protein-packed green peas and dressed with peanut sauce. You'll be feeling better in a flash, just in time to take the world by storm with the vibrant force of nature that is you.

PEANUT-PEA *pasta*

12 ounces **penne**

1½ cups **frozen green peas**

½ cup **unsalted smooth peanut butter**

¼ cup **water, plus more as needed**

1½ tablespoons **reduced-sodium soy sauce or Coconut Aminos**

2 teaspoons **minced garlic**

¼ teaspoon **ground ginger**

1 teaspoon **agave nectar**

1 teaspoon **light brown sugar**

Pinch **cayenne** (optional)

¼ cup **sliced scallion greens**

I know you're exhausted, but you can do this. Rally your inner troops and prepare the pasta according to the package directions. During the last 3 minutes of cooking, add the peas. Drain the pasta and peas in a colander and set aside. Take a deep breath.

While the pasta cooks, combine the peanut butter, water, soy sauce, garlic, ginger, agave nectar, brown sugar, and optional cayenne in a food processor. Process until smooth and creamy, stopping as needed to scrape down the work bowl with a rubber spatula. If the mixture is too thick, add up to ¼ cup of water, 1 tablespoon at a time, until the desired consistency is achieved.

Put the pasta and peas in a medium serving bowl. Add the peanut sauce and scallion greens and mix until the pasta is coated.

Are you still alive? Good, because there's a party in a bowl, and you're invited. Now sit down and take a load off. Enjoy your peanutty pasta, and bring yourself back to the land of the living with a generous dollop of vim and a whole lotta verve.

Per serving: 545 calories, 22 g protein, 18 g fat (3 g sat), 83 g carbohydrates, 439 mg sodium, 33 mg calcium, 129 g fiber

VARIATIONS

- For a protein boost, add Tofu Gone Wild (page 75) or some cubed cooked tempeh (see Baba's Tempeh Sandwich, page 86).
- Instead of peanut sauce, toss the pasta and peas with Hot Mess Dressing (page 121) or Cheeky Sauce (see variation, page 122).
- Instead of the peas, add one 15-ounce can of salt-free beans, rinsed and drained. I recommend chickpeas—or anything that reminds you of the hot chick that you are.

DRESS UP
AND GET SAUCY, SISTER

Who needs store-bought salad dressing? Not me! Not you! Not ever again! Not now that this ever-so-simple, ever-so-tasty balsamic vinaigrette is a vital part of your culinary repertoire. Bid that bottled dressing bye-bye and say hello to the vitality that comes with something freshly made. And yes, you may get fresh with me anytime you like.

VITAL *vinaigrette*

½ cup **extra-virgin olive oil**

¼ cup **balsamic vinegar**

2 teaspoons **Dijon mustard**

½ teaspoon **dried basil**

Pinch **salt**

Freshly ground **black pepper**

Measure the oil in a glass measuring cup. Add the vinegar, mustard, basil, and salt. Stir vigorously with a whisk until well blended. Season with pepper to taste, and herald the dawn of a new age that includes freshly made dressing for everyone.

Per 2 tablespoons: 169 calories, 0 g protein, 18 g fat (3 g sat), 2 g carbohydrates, 68 mg sodium, 1 mg calcium, 0 g fiber

TRICKS OF THE TRADE: I adore this dressing tossed with Threesome Salad (page 58). Add the dressing to the salad just before serving, because what's a threesome without some fresh vitality thrown into the mix?

Ah, a recipe named explicitly after me! Aren't you thrilled? From the title alone, you can guess that this salad dressing must be flawless and lawless, just like its audacious namesake. Pour this ginger-maple-mustard dressing over your favorite vegetable salad, or use it as a dip for fresh veggies. What more could you possibly want? Oh, you want that recipe for Mistress Ginger Un-dressing. Don't they all?

mistress ginger DRESSING

½ cup **firm silken tofu**

¼ cup **extra-virgin olive oil**

2 tablespoons **cider vinegar**

2 teaspoons **maple syrup**

1 teaspoon **Dijon mustard**

¼ teaspoon **ground ginger**

Pinch **salt**

Combine all the ingredients in a food processor. Process until as smooth as Mistress Ginger. (That means *very* smooth.)

Per 2 tablespoons: 77 calories, 1 g protein, 7 g fat (1 g sat), 1 g carbohydrates, 30 mg sodium, 7 mg calcium, 0 g fiber

MISTRESS GINGER VINAIGRETTE: For a not-so-creamy Mistress Ginger Dressing, omit the silken tofu and whisk the remaining ingredients together in a small bowl. You'll have a lovely vinaigrette, perfect for a Threesome Salad (page 58).

With just three ingredients, this dressing is supremely simple but tasty beyond belief. Ume plum vinegar is both sour and salty, a perfect complement to the pleasingly bitter and full-bodied tahini. This rich-tasting but altogether healthy dressing begs to be drizzled on Mondo Salade (page 60), Threesome Salad (page 58), or Flaming Stir-Fry (page 106), or used in place of the peanut sauce in Peanut-Pea Pasta (page 116). Go on, drizzle me! It'll be our little secret.

drizzle me DRESSING

¼ cup **tahini**

1½ teaspoons **ume plum vinegar**

½ cup **water**

In a small bowl or measuring cup, stir together the tahini and the vinegar using a fork or whisk. Gradually stir in the water, 1 tablespoon at a time, until a drizzle-worthy consistency is reached.

Per 2 tablespoons: 64 calories, 2 g protein, 6 g fat (1 g sat), 2 g carbohydrates, 288 mg sodium, 13 mg calcium, 0 g fiber

TRICKS OF THE TRADE: I adore tahini and have for years. In fact, I think we qualify as a common-law married couple at this point. Note that some brands of tahini are much thicker than others and will require that you use more water to achieve a creamy and easily pourable dressing. Be sensitive to the needs of your tahini, and treat it like you'd treat your significant other, minus the vigorous whisking (unless you like that kind of thing).

This warm tahini-miso dressing is just perfect for a handful like you. You can splash, pour, drip, or drizzle it over almost anything you like. Make a mess, as I know you're wont to do, with your broken heel, crooked wig, and public meltdowns. Or is that just me having the public meltdowns? Well, if you're anything like the hot mess that I am, you'll enjoy the stick-to-your-ribs creaminess that this dressing lends to many dishes. I find that the flavor works especially well when drizzled over a Flaming Stir-Fry (page 106). Or think of it as a sauce and use it to replace the peanut sauce in Peanut-Pea Pasta (page 116). Hot messes unite!

hot mess DRESSING

1 cup **water**

2 tablespoons **miso** (barley, sweet white, or chickpea)

½ cup **tahini**

Heat the water in a small saucepan or a tea kettle over medium-high heat until almost boiling. Remove from the heat—and try not to spill the boiling water all over yourself, as we hot messes are inclined to do.

Mix the miso and ½ cup of the water in a small bowl until the miso is diluted. Add the tahini and mix. Gradually stir in additional water just until the desired consistency is reached, or until you make a hot mess.

Per 2 tablespoons: 68 calories, 2 g protein, 6 g fat (1 g sat), 3 g carbohydrates, 128 mg sodium, 17 mg calcium, 1 g fiber

"But I could never live without cheese!" Famous last words, thanks to recipes such as this one. Add a dollop of Cheeky Spread to Buddy's Burrito Bowl (page 115), use it to make a What-a-Tease Sandwich (page 85), or dip your Hot Tots (page 74) in it. Chilled, the spread will thicken somewhat and can be relished on crackers, sandwiches, or crunchy raw vegetables. Feel free to get cheeky anytime you like and make regular old cheese a thing of the past.

cheeky SPREAD

1 cup **plain unsweetened nondairy milk**

½ cup **raw cashews**

¼ cup **nutritional yeast**

2 teaspoons **cornstarch**

¼ teaspoon **garlic powder**

¼ teaspoon **onion powder**

1 teaspoon **salt**

1 teaspoon **freshly squeezed lemon juice**

Put the nondairy milk, cashews, nutritional yeast, cornstarch, garlic powder, onion powder, and salt in a blender. Process on high speed until smooth, and ponder what cheeky thing you might say the next time you hear someone declare that they couldn't live without cheese.

Transfer the blended mixture to a medium saucepan. Simmer over medium heat, stirring constantly, until beginning to thicken and bubble, 5 to 7 minutes. While you stir, practice your new cheeky line: "I too was once in a committed, codependent relationship with cheese. We parted ways amicably, around the same time I met cashews. Oh, cashews just swept me off my feet. Now we're inseparable, and I don't even think about cheese."

Remove from the heat, stir in the lemon juice, and share your Cheeky Spread and your cheeky comeback with as many cheese addicts as you can find.

Store leftover Cheeky Spread in a tightly sealed container in the refrigerator and use within 1 week.

Per 2 tablespoons: 54 calories, 2 g protein, 4 g fat (1 g sat), 4 g carbohydrates, 309 mg sodium, 43 mg calcium, 1 g fiber

CHEEKY SAUCE: If you desire a cheesy sauce for something like a veganized macaroni and cheese (or as I like to call it, "Mac and Cheek"), prepare Cheeky Spread but omit the cornstarch. You'll have a flavorful sauce that you can pour, drip, or drizzle. Cheeky Sauce will thicken somewhat when chilled. You may then enjoy it as more of a spread than a sauce. Alternatively, reheat the leftovers, gradually adding water until you've once again achieved the saucy consistency of your cheeky dreams.

Shakti is a Sanskrit word meaning "the creative power of the universe." Naturally, I thought it the perfect name for this power-packed spread made from sunflower seeds, red lentils, and an assortment of aromatic spices. Use it as a curried condiment for Baba's Tempeh Sandwich (page 86), a spread for some crispy crackers, or a dip for fresh veggies. However you serve it, Shakti Spread is bound to give you loads of energy with which you can access your own creative power and command center stage at your next song-and-dance extravaganza.

SHAKTI *spread*

½ cup **red lentils, rinsed and drained**

2¼ cups **water**

⅔ cup **raw sunflower seeds**

2 tablespoons **extra-virgin olive oil**

1 teaspoon **reduced-sodium soy sauce or Coconut Aminos**

1 teaspoon **curry powder**

½ teaspoon **salt**

¼ teaspoon **onion powder**

⅛ teaspoon **garlic powder**

⅛ teaspoon **ground cumin**

Pinch **ground coriander**

To begin making this sacred spread, you must enter the realm of the red lentil. But don't be afraid; red lentils are a cinch to prepare. Put the lentils and 2 cups of the water in a medium saucepan and bring to a boil over high heat. Decrease the heat to medium-low, cover, and simmer until the lentils are tender and the water has been absorbed completely, about 15 minutes. Remove from the heat and let sit covered for 5 minutes.

Put the sunflower seeds in a food processor and process until finely ground, about 2 minutes.

Add the lentils, oil, soy sauce, curry powder, salt, onion powder, garlic powder, cumin, and coriander and process for about 3 minutes, until a smooth paste forms.

Continue processing, adding 1 tablespoon of the remaining water at a time, until a creamy and spreadable consistency is reached. Let the spinning of the blade remind you of an ecstatic whirling dervish . . . or twirling showgirl. Whee!

Store leftover Shakti Spread in a tightly sealed container in the refrigerator and use within 1 week.

Per 3 tablespoons: 82 calories, 3 g protein, 6 g fat (1 g sat), 6 g carbohydrates, 130 mg sodium, 10 mg calcium, 3 g fiber

Are you ready to par-tay with some pâté? This mellow mushroom-walnut spread will be the perfect cracker spread or veggie dip for your next chic soiree. Non-vegan pâté is often made from goose liver. I don't know about you, but that doesn't put me in the party mood. My version of this sumptuous spread is truly elegant because it's cruelty-free. Let the geese run free! They have their gaggle, and you have yours. Par-tay with your gaggle of giggly friends, and live it up the vegan way, every day.

par-tay PÂTÉ

1½ tablespoons **extra-virgin olive oil**

1½ cups **diced onions**

4 cups **sliced white button mushrooms**

1 tablespoon **minced garlic**

1 teaspoon **dried marjoram**

½ cup **chopped walnuts**

¾ cup **crumbled firm silken tofu**

1 tablespoon **reduced-sodium soy sauce or Coconut Aminos**

Salt

Freshly ground **black pepper**

This cruelty-free fare is easy to prepare. To begin, heat the oil in a large skillet over medium-high heat. Add the onions and cook, stirring occasionally, until beginning to brown, about 15 minutes. Add the mushrooms and cook, stirring occasionally, until tender, about 5 minutes. Add the garlic and cook, stirring constantly, until fragrant, about 2 minutes. Stir in the marjoram and cook until all the vegetables are very tender, about 1 minute. Remove from the heat and let cool to room temperature.

Put the walnuts in a food processor and process until finely ground. (You'll notice that the walnuts do not cry out in pain when they are whizzed up in the food processor. You can feel good about that.) Add the tofu, vegetable mixture, and soy sauce. Process until well combined, about 3 minutes, stopping as needed to scrape down the work bowl with a rubber spatula. Season with salt and pepper to taste.

Transfer to a storage container and chill for at least 1 hour before serving. Take your pâté to the park for a little picnic and frolic with the geese in good conscience.

Store leftover pâté in a tightly sealed container in the refrigerator and use within 1 week.

Per 2 tablespoons: 70 calories, 2 g protein, 6 g fat (1 g sat), 3 g carbohydrates, 44 mg sodium, 8 mg calcium, 1 g fiber

The piquant flavor and earthy texture of this olive-walnut tapenade will titillate your senses, and don't we all want to be titillated at every possible moment of every stinking day? Or is that just me? Well, while I'm out getting some routine titillation, you can spread this tapenade over crackers or crusty bread, or use it as a chunky dip for carrot sticks, cucumber slices, or other fresh veggies. Be titillated at every moment. Let this be your mantra. (It's a decent alternative to the "Mistress Ginger is the queen of all time" mantra that you've been using.)

TITILLATING *Tapenade*

YIELDS 1 CUP

¾ cup **black olives**

½ cup **walnuts**

¼ cup **pitted kalamata olives**

1 tablespoon **extra-virgin olive oil**

1 tablespoon **freshly squeezed lemon juice**

1 tablespoon **dried parsley**

1 teaspoon **dried thyme**

1 teaspoon **Dijon mustard**

½ teaspoon **dried rosemary, crushed**

½ teaspoon **minced garlic**

Pinch **salt**

Pinch **freshly ground black pepper**

Here we have another one of those incredibly complicated recipes. Prepare yourself by chanting the mantra that I have bestowed upon you: "Be titillated at every moment. Be titillated at every moment. Be titillated at every moment."

Combine all the ingredients in a food processor. Process until just mixed, leaving some chunky texture.

That's it. All that's left is to eat and be titillated. Think you can handle that?

Per 2 tablespoons: 124 calories, 2 g protein, 12 g fat (1 g sat), 3 g carbohydrates, 59 mg sodium, 1 mg calcium, 1 g fiber

One, two, cha-cha-cha. Three, four, hear me roar. This tangy, sweet-and-spicy mango spread will make you want to put on a ruffle skirt, do the cha-cha, and then roar like the sexy beast you are. I guarantee it. Home-made jam was never so quick and easy. This version is perfect for Baba's Tempeh Sandwich (page 86), but it can also be spread on your morning toast alongside a bit of Hell's Kitchen Scramble (page 30). Do you mind if I cha-cha my way into your heart with this chutney? I didn't think so.

cha-cha-cha CHUTNEY

1 cup **peeled and diced mango** (about 1 large mango)

2 tablespoons **minced scallion**

1 tablespoon **raisins**

1 tablespoon **cider vinegar**

2 teaspoons **agave nectar**

½ teaspoon **minced garlic**

¼ teaspoon **dry mustard**

¼ teaspoon **ground ginger**

Pinch **red pepper flakes**

Cha-cha your way over to the stove. Combine all the ingredients in a small saucepan. Bring to a simmer over medium-high heat. Stir, cover, decrease the heat to medium-low, and simmer for 10 minutes. Remove from the heat and let sit covered for 5 minutes.

Transfer the mixture to a food processor and pulse a few times until partially blended. "Pulse, pulse, cha-cha-cha. Pulse, pulse, cha-cha-cha. Pulse, pulse, cha-cha-cha."

Store leftover Cha-Cha-Cha Chutney in a tightly sealed container in the refrigerator and use within 1 week.

Per 3 tablespoons: 47 calories, 0 g protein, 0 g fat (0 g sat), 12 g carbohydrates, 2 mg sodium, 8 mg calcium, 1 g fiber

You guessed it. I knew a man named Alfredo, and he taught me how to make this sauce. Now hold up! Before you think you've caught on to my shtick, listen here. Alfredo was not my lover; he was my teacher, my dance teacher. He taught me many of my hottest dance moves when I was but a fledgling showgirl, and he said that this sauce would help to fuel my dancing feet. He was right! Made with a few wholesome ingredients but packed with rich, savory flavor, this vegan version of a classic Alfredo sauce will get you out on the dance floor, cutting a rug and tearing it up, especially when it's served over Bodacious Tortelloni (page 102) or another carb-o-licious pasta.

ALFREDO'S *sauce*

1 cup **plain unsweetened nondairy milk**

¼ cup **raw cashews**

½ teaspoon **salt**

½ teaspoon **Dijon mustard**

2 tablespoons **vegan buttery spread**

2 teaspoons **minced garlic**

Put the nondairy milk, cashews, salt, and mustard in a blender and process on high speed until smooth. That reminds me, I know a dance step called the Blender. It's been illegal in five states ever since I took out the front row of an audience in Des Moines. But I'll show it to ya if you've signed a liability waiver.

Heat the vegan buttery spread in a large saucepan over medium-high heat. Add the garlic and cook, stirring constantly, until fragrant, about 2 minutes. Add the cashew mixture and cook, stirring constantly, until thickened, about 7 minutes. That reminds me, I know another dance step called the Constant Stir. I don't dare do it unless I've had a couple of Dramamine first. And it's really a recipe for disaster when I try to do the Blender immediately following the Constant Stir. Bad things happen.

But you know what's *not* a recipe for disaster? This recipe for Alfredo's Sauce. When your sauce is thick and creamy, remove it from the heat and pour it over your pasta for some high-octane dancing fuel.

Per ¼ cup: 100 calories, 2 g protein, 9 g fat (2 g sat), 3 g carbohydrates, 388 mg sodium, 120 mg calcium, 1 g fiber

Pesto is comfort food with class. For a good time, toss it with pasta, such as Bodacious Tortelloni (page 102), spread it on toast to make bruschetta, use it on pizza as an alternative to marinara, or drizzle it over grilled vegetables. This gorgeous green sauce is a cinch to prepare but looks so fancy. You can easily impress a new lover with this one. Ta-dah! Now kiss me, and let's get this party started.

PRESTO *pesto*

2 cups **stemmed fresh basil, firmly packed**

½ cup **walnuts**

2 teaspoons **minced garlic**

1 teaspoon **freshly squeezed lemon juice**, plus more as needed

½ teaspoon **salt**, plus more as needed

¼ teaspoon **dried thyme**

⅓ cup **extra-virgin olive oil**

Freshly ground **black pepper**

Combine the basil, walnuts, garlic, lemon juice, salt, and thyme in a food processor. Pulse until just mixed and still chunky. Stop as needed to scrape down the work bowl with a rubber spatula.

Process the mixture while adding the oil in a steady stream. Stop processing as needed to scrape down the work bowl. Continue processing until completely mixed but still a little chunky. Pesto should be mostly smooth with just the right amount of stubbly texture, like my men.

Season with additional lemon juice, salt, and pepper to taste. The flavor of the pesto by itself should be very bold, also like my men. Wow, I never realized how much my men and my pesto have in common. That must explain why I can't get enough of either.

Per 2 tablespoons: 129 calories, 1 g protein, 14 g fat (2 g sat), 1 g carbohydrates, 143 mg sodium, 16 mg calcium, 1 g fiber

I'm not one to toot my own horn, but, toot, toot—this guacamole kicks ass. I really can't take all the credit since Mother Nature did most of the work. Take some fresh ingredients, mash them up in a bowl, and have your way with them. Dip your chips, spread your bread, or throw a dollop onto Buddy's Burrito Bowl (page 115). Buddy won't mind. In fact, I know he likes a dollop every now and then.

kickass GUACAMOLE

YIELDS 1 ½ CUPS

3 **ripe avocados**

3 tablespoons **diced onion**

3 tablespoons **diced seeded tomato**

3 tablespoons **finely chopped fresh cilantro**

2 tablespoons **freshly squeezed lime juice**

1 tablespoon **minced garlic**

1 tablespoon **minced jalapeño chile**

Salt

Freshly ground **black pepper**

Here are Mother Nature's instructions for making gorgeous guac. I am just the messenger. She said, and I quote, "Mash the avocados in a medium bowl with a fork. Stir in the onion, tomato, cilantro, lime juice, garlic, and chile. Season with salt and pepper to taste. Cover and refrigerate until ready to serve." Mother Nature cuts to the chase, doesn't she?

Use within 2 days, as if that will be an issue.

Per 2 tablespoons: 86 calories, 1 g protein, 7 g fat (1 g sat), 6 g carbohydrates, 5 mg sodium, 17 mg calcium, 4 g fiber

I thought I'd try my hand at haiku poetry: *Not* a ricotta
Instead, *tofu* ricotta
Nottaricotta

Does it work? I think-a-notta. But you wanna know what does work? This recipe. It works to replace ricotta cheese in the event of an emergency veganizing, as in the case of Lip-Smackin' Lasagna (page 104) or Bodacious Tortelloni (page 102).

 # *notta* RICOTTA

YIELDS 2¼ CUPS

1 pound **firm tofu**

⅓ cup **vegan mayonnaise**

2 teaspoons **freshly squeezed lemon juice**

1 tablespoon **nutritional yeast**

1 teaspoon **dried basil**

¾ teaspoon **salt**

¼ teaspoon **dried oregano**

¼ teaspoon **dried thyme**

¼ teaspoon **garlic powder**

¼ teaspoon **onion powder**

Haikus aside, let's replace that ricotta in a few easy steps. First, drain and rinse the tofu. Pat dry with a paper towel and set aside.

Second, put the vegan mayonnaise, lemon juice, nutritional yeast, basil, salt, oregano, thyme, garlic powder, and onion powder in a medium bowl and stir until well combined.

Now crumble the tofu into the bowl and stir until well combined. Store leftover Nottaricotta in a tightly sealed container in the refrigerator and use within 1 week.

Aren't you relieved that I didn't try to deliver the recipe instructions in haiku form? I sure as hell am.

Per ¼ cup: 137 calories, 9 g protein, 10 g fat (1 g sat), 2 g carbohydrates, 60 mg sodium, 66 mg calcium, 0 g fiber

Get ready. You are about to have your mind blown! (I said your *mind*!) With one stroke of genius, your Mistress has redefined what it means to be real. Don't think of this cream cheese alternative as "fake" cream cheese, and don't expect some shoddy knockoff that you'll have to pretend to enjoy. No compromises here! Prepare to love it for what it is: pure perfection. The coconut oil imparts a subtle coconut flavor, and the ground cashews give a creamy density. Simply smear this cleverly conceived concoction on a bagel, or go all out and use it for Fancy Cucumber Sandwiches (page 94), Classy Crêpes (page 34), or even Coconutty Ginger Cheesecake (page 150). Dream big. This vegan cream cheese is for reals!

coconutty CREAM CHEESE

1½ tablespoons **coconut oil**

¼ cup **raw cashews**

¾ cup **crumbled firm silken tofu**

1 tablespoon **freshly squeezed lemon juice**

¼ teaspoon **salt**, plus more if desired (see Tricks of the Trade)

Aiming for pure perfection? Coconut oil is a very good place to start. If the coconut oil is solidified, warm it in a small saucepan over very low heat until liquefied.

Now for the cashews. They have a kind of perfection all their own. Process the cashews in a blender on high speed until very finely ground.

Put the coconut oil, ground cashews, tofu, lemon juice, and salt in a food processor. Process until smooth, about 3 minutes, stopping as needed to scrape down the work bowl with a rubber spatula. Girl, you better whirl it and twirl it. Taste and add more salt if desired.

Transfer to a storage container and chill for at least 3 hours, until firm. (This is when the magic happens.)

Store leftover Coconutty Cream Cheese in a tightly sealed container in the refrigerator and use within 1 week.

Per 2 tablespoons: 57 calories, 3 g protein, 4 g fat (3 g sat), 2 g carbohydrates, 98 mg sodium, 10 mg calcium, 0 g fiber

TRICKS OF THE TRADE: If you're making Coconutty Cream Cheese to spread on a bagel, adding some extra salt will make your schmear simply divoon. Skip the extra salt if you're preparing the cream cheese to use in other recipes, such as Classy Crêpes (page 34) or Coconutty Ginger Cheesecake (page 150).

Friends of Dorothy, this one's for you. Just click your six-inch heels together a few times and say a little prayer. Pray for a maple-sweetened raspberry sauce that you can use for breakfast or dessert. Pour it over Wicked Waffles (page 31), Classy Crêpes (page 34), or Coconutty Ginger Cheesecake (page 150). "There's no place like Ginger's kitchen, there's no place like Ginger's kitchen, there's no place like Ginger's kitchen . . ." Damn straight!

 # *ruby-red* SYRUP

1 cup **fresh raspberries**

½ cup **maple syrup**

2 teaspoons **cornstarch**

When you've finished frollicking down the yellow brick road, put the raspberries and maple syrup in a medium saucepan over medium heat. Cook, stirring occasionally, until the raspberries begin to break down, about 5 minutes.

Stir with a whisk until the mixture is somewhat smooth. Add the cornstarch and increase the heat to medium-high. Cook, stirring constantly, until the mixture thickens and bubbles, about 3 minutes.

Remove from the heat and let cool for at least 5 minutes before serving.

Ruby-Red Syrup should be kept in a tightly sealed container in the refrigerator and used within 1 week. Ruby-red slippers should never be taken off your feet, unless you want to be at the mercy of some flying monkeys. It's up to you.

Per 2 tablespoons: 61 calories, 0 g protein, 0 g fat (0 g sat), 15 g carbohydrates, 0 mg sodium, 24 mg calcium, 1 g fiber

PUT A LITTLE SUGAR
IN MY BOWL

Ah, here it is, what you've all been waiting for: a recipe with Ginger as the main event! Sink your teeth into my soft and chewy gingersnatch. I'm talking about cookies, you fiend! These gingery oatmeal cookies sparkle with a light sugar coating. They'll lead you headfirst into my personal Kingdom of Sweets, where you'll find me perched on my throne as the reigning queen of sugar and spice and everything nice . . . and everything naughty.

gingersnatch COOKIES

1½ cups **whole wheat pastry flour**

¾ cups **rolled oats**

1 teaspoon **baking soda**

1 teaspoon **ground ginger**

½ teaspoon **baking powder**

½ teaspoon **ground cinnamon**

¼ teaspoon **ground cloves**

¼ teaspoon **salt**

2 teaspoons **Ener-G Egg Replacer**

2 tablespoons **warm water**

1 cup **granulated sugar**

½ cup **vegan buttery spread**

¼ cup **blackstrap molasses**

1 teaspoon **vanilla extract**

All hands on deck. Serious gingersnatch action (also known as "gingersnac tion") is about to transpire. Preheat the oven to 350 degrees F. Lightly oil baking sheet or line it with parchment paper.

Mix the flour, oats, baking soda, ginger, baking powder, cinnamon cloves, and salt in a medium bowl.

Combine the egg replacer with the water in a food processor and proces until frothy, about 3 minutes. How are you doing with the gingersnaction so far?

Put ¾ cup of the sugar and the vegan buttery spread in a large bow and mix using an electric mixer. Add the molasses, vanilla extract, and eg replacer. Stir the dry mixture into the wet mixture using a wooden spoon to form a dough.

Roll the dough into 24 balls, each about 1 inch in diameter. Roll eacl ball in the remaining ¼ cup of the sugar to create a thin coating and put o the prepared baking sheet.

Bake for 12 minutes. Let rest on the baking sheet for 3 to 5 minutes before transferring to a cooling rack.

Gingersnatch Cookies will stay fresh in a tightly sealed container at room temperature for 1 week or in the refrigerator for 2 weeks.

Congratulations! You've had your first experience with gingersnaction How was it for you? You know what they say: "Once you go gingersnatch you never go back."

Per cookie: 107 calories, 1 g protein, 4 g fat (1 g sat), 17 g carbohydrates, 118 mg sodium, 34 mg calcium, 1 g fiber

I am convinced that chocolate chip cookies were put here on earth to uplift and inspire us all so that we may reach new heights of consciousness. They have always been my go-to dessert, which probably explains why I am such an exceptionally evolved soul. Since I eat chocolate chip cookies so often, I wanted to develop my own recipe for the classic cookie that would be simple and wholesome but still capable of setting my metaphysical energy centers ablaze. These Chakra Chip Cookies pass the test with flying colors. They satisfy the sweet tooth and might even inspire world peace. Well, if nothing else, they inspire my inner peace, even if just for a moment.

chakra chip COOKIES

1 cup **whole wheat pastry flour**

1¼ teaspoons **baking powder**

¼ teaspoon **baking soda**

¼ teaspoon **salt**

¼ cup **coconut oil**

¼ cup **light brown sugar, firmly packed**

¼ cup **maple syrup**

1¼ teaspoons **vanilla extract**

¼ cup **nondairy semisweet chocolate chips** (heaping!)

If you're a cookie monster like me, preheat the oven to 350 degrees F. Lightly oil a baking sheet or line it with parchment paper.

Mix the flour, baking powder, baking soda, and salt in a large bowl.

If the coconut oil has solidified, warm it in a small saucepan over low heat. Once the oil has liquefied, remove it from the heat. Add the brown sugar, maple syrup, and vanilla extract and whisk until well combined. (If the oil is still warm and has made the wet mixture warm, let cool to room temperature before adding to the dry mixture so you don't melt your chocolate chips before you even get them into the oven.)

Add the wet mixture to the dry mixture. Mix until just combined to make a dough. Fold in the chocolate chips.

Roll the dough into 12 balls, each about 1½ inches in diameter and put on the prepared baking sheet.

Bake for 11 minutes. Let rest on the baking sheet for 2 minutes before transferring to a cooling rack. Cool for at least 5 minutes before eating. I read somewhere, probably in some ancient scripture, that one chakra chip cookie eaten while still warm from the oven is capable of inducing spontaneous enlightenment, or was it spontaneous orgasm? Wait, maybe I read that in *Cosmo*. Either way, I'm going to have to test this theory about a dozen times.

Per cookie: 158 calories, 1 g protein, 7 g fat (5 g sat), 24 g carbohydrates, 111 mg sodium, 53 mg calcium, 1 g fiber

Besides being vegan, my succulent balls have no refined sugar or gluten in them. These date-nut morsels could serve as a healthy dessert option, a power-packed midday snack, or even an on-the-go breakfast. I've said it before, and I'll say it again—you are going to love my balls!

GINGER'S *balls*

½ cup **raw cashews**

1 cup **pitted medjool dates** (about 10 dates)

1 tablespoon **peeled and minced fresh ginger**

⅛ teaspoon **ground cardamom**

¼ cup **hempseeds or unsweetened shredded dried coconut**

Put the cashews in a food processor and process until coarsely ground. Add the dates, ginger, and cardamom and process until well combined.

Roll the mixture into 1-inch balls. Put the hempseeds on a plate and roll each ball in the hempseeds. Shake off the excess so that a thin coating remains.

Store in a tightly sealed container in the refrigerator and enjoy my balls within 2 weeks.

Per ball: 121 calories, 3 g protein, 4 g fat (1 g sat), 20 g carbohydrates, 1 mg sodium, 22 mg calcium, 2 g fiber

TRICKS OF THE TRADE: On the subject of dates, I recommend not moving in with a new lover until you've had at least ten dates. That's my personal rule: ten dates or two months—whichever comes first.

These nut-filled pastries evoke an old world vibe and connect me to the ways of my ancestors. When I'm rolling out the dough, I imagine I'm an old Slovakian lady wearing a headscarf, or babooshka, tied under my chin. Make these spectacular Slovak cookies on a cold winter's day, when the snow is piling up outside and you've got the time to roll out the dough at one-hour intervals, which is the secret to making

BABOOSHKA *bundles*

FIRST DOUGH

1 tablespoon **Ener-G Egg Replacer**

3 tablespoons **cold water**, plus more as needed

⅓ cup **nondairy sour cream**

1 cup **chilled unbleached all-purpose white flour**, plus more for rolling the dough

SECOND DOUGH

1 cup **chilled unbleached all-purpose white flour**

1 cup **vegan buttery spread**

Put on your babooshka and some kind of old-school apron to shield your pinstripe pantsuit.

To make the first dough, put the egg replacer and water in a food processor. Process until thickened and frothy, about 3 minutes. Add the nondairy sour cream and process until well combined, about 1 minute.

Sift 1 cup of the flour into a large bowl. Add the sour cream mixture and stir until a dough begins to form. If the mixture doesn't clump, add just enough additional cold water, about 1 tablespoon, so that it does. Lightly knead the dough, form it into a ball, wrap with plastic wrap, and chill for 30 minutes.

When the first dough is nearly chilled, prepare the second dough. Put the flour in a large bowl. Cut the vegan buttery spread into the flour using a pastry blender or fork until large lumps form; the dough should be soft and spreadable.

Put the first dough on a floured surface and roll into a ⅛-inch-thick circle, about 12 inches in diameter. Spread the second dough evenly over the first dough with a rubber spatula.

Here's where the fun begins, and you get to repeat it four times!

One: Fold the dough as many times as possible, wrap with plastic wrap, and chill for 1 hour.

Two: Roll out the dough on a floured surface and fold as before. Wrap with plastic wrap and chill for 1 hour.

Three: Again (stay with me), roll out the dough and fold as before. Wrap with plastic wrap and chill for 1 hour.

it delectably flaky. Then present this labor of love at your next holiday gathering. I guarantee the finished product will garner some oohs and aahs, and if you wear a babooshka, you're likely to get a few other reactions as well. (Just don't expect too many hot come-ons.)

FILLING AND TOPPING

¼ cup **whole flaxseeds**

1½ cups **water**

1 cup **pecans or walnuts, finely chopped**

1 cup **sugar**

1 teaspoon **vanilla extract**

1 teaspoon **freshly squeezed lemon juice**

½ cup **powdered sugar**

Four: Now, one last time, roll out the dough and fold as before. Wrap with plastic wrap and chill for 1 hour. Don't say I didn't warn you! This dough rolling isn't for the faint of heart. Those babooshka-wearing women were tough old broads. Now you be one too!

While the dough chills for the last hour, prepare the filling. Put the flaxseeds and water in a small saucepan and bring to a boil over high heat. Decrease the heat to medium and simmer until thick, about 7 minutes. Put a fine-mesh strainer over a small bowl or measuring cup. Pour the flax mixture through the strainer. Discard the flaxseeds and set aside the thick flax goop.

Put the pecans and sugar in a medium bowl. Stir in the vanilla extract and lemon juice. Add ⅓ cup of the flax goop and stir until well combined. Let the mixture sit for at least 20 minutes to thicken slightly.

When you're ready to begin assembling the Babooshka Bundles, preheat the oven to 375 degrees F. Lightly oil a baking sheet or line it with parchment paper.

Roll out the dough until it is ⅛ inch thick. (Okay, I lied before. This is *truly* the last time!) Cut the dough into 2½-inch squares. Spread 2 teaspoons of the filling on each square and fold two opposite corners of the dough up over the filling. Moisten one of the corners with a dab of water and bring the other corner over to glue it down and seal the bundle. Arrange 18 of these darling bundles on the prepared baking sheet.

Bake for 22 to 25 minutes, or until golden brown. While the first batch bakes, prepare another 18 bundles for the oven. Remove the first batch from the oven and transfer to a cooling rack. Bake the second batch, remove from the oven, and transfer to a cooling rack. Let all the bundles cool for at least 1 hour.

Once all the bundles are cool, arrange them on a serving platter. Just before serving, lightly sprinkle the powdered sugar over the bundles using a sifter, and then feed your labor of love to your loved ones. (Babooshka optional.)

Store leftover Babooshka Bundles in a tightly sealed container in the refrigerator and use within 2 weeks.

Per serving: 125 calories, 1 g protein, 8 g fat (1 g sat), 11 g carbohydrates, 54 mg sodium, 10 mg calcium, 1 g fiber

TRICKS OF THE TRADE: I'm just a traveling showgirl, but I've managed to learn a thing or two about achieving the perfect pastry. Keep it chill, man! I'm not a chemist and can't tell you how it works. All I know is that if you want a light and flaky pastry, you should keep your ingredients chilled whenever you're not using them.

Papa, can you hear me? I'm wondering if there is a twelve-step program for potato candy. That is to say, a program for someone who can't stop eating potato candy, not for the potato candy itself. Although, maybe potato candy should get some group therapy too. After all, its days are numbered. You think this is crazy

papa's POTATO CANDY

YIELDS ABOUT 40 PIECES

½ cup **peeled and cubed potato**

½ teaspoon **vanilla extract**

Pinch **salt**

1 (16-ounce) package **powdered sugar**

½ cup **salted smooth peanut butter, chilled** (see Tricks of the Trade)

Hi. My name is Ginger, and I'm addicted to Potato Candy.

Put about 2 cups of water in a medium saucepan. Bring to a boil over medium-high heat. Add the potato and cook until easily pierced with a fork, about 7 minutes. Remove from the heat and let the potato rest in the saucepan 3 minutes longer. Drain and let cool completely.

Put the potato in a large bowl. Using an electric mixer, beat the potato until completely mashed. Add the vanilla extract and salt. Mix again until well blended.

Gradually beat the powdered sugar into the potato mixture, about ½ cup at a time. Add as much of the sugar as necessary to create a thick dough. (A little mashed potato can absorb a lot of sugar, much in the same way that I can absorb a lot of sugar, especially when delivered in the form of sweet nothings whispered in my ear.)

Divide the dough into two balls. Wrap each dough ball in plastic wrap and chill for at least 30 minutes.

Sprinkle a handful of powdered sugar on the countertop. With a rolling pin, roll one of the dough balls into a rectangular shape about ¼ inch thick and 6 inches wide by 8 inches long. (Sprinkle the dough and the countertop frequently with powdered sugar to prevent sticking.) Spread half the peanut butter in a thin layer over the dough.

Tightly roll up the dough lengthwise to create a pinwheel effect with the peanut butter as the filling. Repeat with the remaining dough and peanut butter. Wrap both rolls in waxed paper and refrigerate for at least 1 hour, until firm.

talk, but just you wait until you make this old-fashioned confection. You too will be addicted to these peanut-buttery sugar bombs. Jacked up on sugar, you'll be spouting nonsense to passersby at the nearest bus station that you can find. Warning: Proceed with caution, a slew of hungry friends, and a reverence for moderation.

When ready to serve, slice the roll into ¼-inch-thick pinwheels. Store leftover pinwheel slices in a tightly sealed container in the refrigerator and use within 1 week, which as I mentioned before won't be hard to do. In fact, the bigger challenge will be making this potato candy last even a day.

Papa don't preach. I made up my mind. I'm keeping my potato candy . . . all to myself!

Per piece (based on 40 pieces): 74 calories, 1 g protein, 2 g fat (0.3 g sat), 14 g carbohydrates, 15 mg sodium, 2 mg calcium, 0 g fiber

TRICKS OF THE TRADE: Chilled peanut butter works well for this, since it will be a little stiffer and won't squish out as you roll it. By the way, "squish out" is a technical term in highfalutin culinary circles.

Get ready for your taste buds to get seriously serviced. This melt-in-your-mouth fruit crisp is ready, willing, and able. Serve warm, with Tenderly Whipped Topping (page 161) or nondairy ice cream to heighten the experience. Who would have guessed that a freaking fruit crisp would be the love of your life—or even just a thrilling one-night stand? Oh, it can, and it will.

APPLE-BLUEBERRY *crisp*

3 cups **apples, peeled and sliced** (¼ inch thick)

2 cups **fresh or frozen blueberries**

1 cup plus 2 tablespoons **whole wheat pastry flour**

¼ cup **light brown sugar, packed**

¾ cup **sugar**

1 teaspoon **baking powder**

½ teaspoon **ground cinnamon**

½ teaspoon **salt**

2 teaspoons **Ener-G Egg Replacer**

3 tablespoons **warm water**

½ cup **vegan buttery spread, melted**

The best way to initiate a thrilling one-night stand is to simply turn up the heat, and then get things good and lubricated. In other words, preheat the oven to 350 degrees F and coat a 6-cup casserole dish with vegan buttery spread.

Time to get fruity. Mix the apples and blueberries in the casserole dish.

Mix 2 tablespoons of the flour with the brown sugar in a small bowl. Sprinkle over the fruit and stir gently until the fruit is evenly coated.

Sift the remaining 1 cup of the flour into a medium bowl and stir in the sugar, baking powder, cinnamon, and salt until well combined.

Put the egg replacer and water in a food processor and process until frothy, about 3 minutes. Using a fork or pastry blender, cut the frothy mixture into the dry mixture. Sprinkle evenly over the fruit and drizzle with the melted vegan buttery spread.

Bake uncovered for 1 hour until golden brown and bubbly. Let cool for 10 minutes before servicing your overeager taste buds.

Store leftover crisp (if there is such a thing) in a tightly sealed container in the refrigerator and use within 1 week. Chances are, however, that fruity crisp will be gone when you wake up in the morning. Damn those fly-by-night romances!

Per serving: 250 calories, 2 g protein, 12 g fat (3 g sat), 36 g carbohydrates, 290 mg sodium, 74 mg calcium, 4 g fiber

These miniature pumpkin pies are as easy as pie to make and so damn cute you won't know what to do with yourself. Each of your dinner guests will get a mini-pie, so there won't be any holiday bickering over who gets the biggest slice, who gets the last slice, who slept with my boyfriend. You can avoid one of those typical Thanksgiving brawls, the hairpulling, the fisticuffs, the death threats, with these precious single servings. Who doesn't love pumpkin pie? And who slept with my boyfriend? Or better I should ask, who *hasn't* slept with him?

LILLIPUTIAN *pumpkin pies*

YIELDS 6 PETITE PIES

1½ cups **graham cracker crumbs**

¼ cup **coconut oil, liquefied**

1 (12-ounce) package **firm silken tofu, drained and crumbled** (about 1½ cups)

1 (15-ounce) can **pumpkin purée** (about 1¾ cups)

½ cup **maple syrup**

¼ cup **light brown sugar, firmly packed**

2 teaspoons **ground cinnamon**

¼ teaspoon **ground cloves**

¼ teaspoon **ground nutmeg**

¼ teaspoon **ground ginger**

1 teaspoon **vanilla extract**

Tenderly Whipped Topping (page 161)

Pumpkin pie. You know you want it. Now come and get it.

First, have six 4½-inch ramekins ready to go. Next, prepare the crust. Put the graham cracker crumbs and oil in a medium bowl. Stir until well combined.

Put ¼ cup of the graham cracker mixture into each ramekin. Using your hands, press the mixture down to form a crust to cover the bottom. Chill for 30 minutes.

Preheat the oven to 350 degrees F.

To make the pie filling, put the tofu in a food processor and process until smooth, about 2 minutes. Add the pumpkin purée, maple syrup, brown sugar, cinnamon, cloves, nutmeg, ginger, and vanilla extract. Process until well combined, stopping as needed to scrape down the work bowl with a rubber spatula.

Divide the batter equally among the ramekins. Arrange the ramekins on a baking sheet and bake for 45 to 50 minutes, until the tops of the pies are golden brown and the centers don't jiggle much. (I usually appreciate jiggling, but not in the case of pumpkin pie.)

Transfer to a cooling rack and let cool for 30 minutes at room temperature. Chill for at least 1 hour before serving.

Just before sharing these treats with your holiday brood, top each pie with a generous ¼-cup dollop of Tenderly Whipped Topping. Be sure to measure each dollop equally, lest you all start bickering about who got the most topping. Before you know it, you'll have your Aunt Edna in a headlock, the twin cousins will be working tag-team strategies, and your little sister will have climbed onto the credenza, ready to launch a body slam. Avoid this sordid scenario at all costs.

Per pie (with whipped topping): 533 calories, 6 g protein, 25 g fat (19 g sat), 73 g carbohydrates, 118 mg sodium, 88 mg calcium, 3 g fiber

Some might say marriage is only between a man and a woman. I disagree. Peanut butter and chocolate have been happily married since the beginning of time. This no-bake treat proves it.

Tie-the-knot CHOCOLATE–PEANUT BUTTER PIE

YIELDS 12 SERVINGS

1 cup **nondairy cream cheese, softened**

1 cup **unsalted smooth peanut butter**

1 cup **sugar**

1 teaspoon **vanilla extract**

1 (15-ounce) can **full-fat coconut milk, chilled for 6 to 8 hours**

1 prepared 9-inch **vegan graham cracker pie crust**

⅓ cup **nondairy milk**

⅔ cup **nondairy semisweet chocolate chips**

2 tablespoons **vegan buttery spread, softened**

Per serving: 422 calories, 7 g protein, 28 g fat (10 g sat), 41 g carbohydrates, 189 mg sodium, 38 mg calcium, 2 g fiber

Dearly beloved, we have gathered here to make a pie. Using an electric mixer, blend the nondairy cream cheese, peanut butter, sugar, and vanilla extract in a large bowl until well combined. Rinse and dry the beaters.

Remove the coconut milk from the fridge, but do not shake the can. (When chilled, the cream from the coconut milk rises to the top.) Gently turn the can upside down and carefully remove the lid. Pour the watery liquid into a storage container and reserve for other purposes (see Tricks of the Trade, page 161). Scoop the coconut cream from the can and put it in a large bowl. Using the electric mixer, beat the coconut cream on high until fluffy, about 5 minutes.

Fold 1 cup of the coconut cream into the peanut butter mixture. Using the electric mixer, blend on low speed until smooth. Scoop the mixture into the pie crust, smooth the top with a rubber spatula, and chill for at least 2 hours.

Heat the nondairy milk in a small saucepan over medium heat just until it begins to steam and bubble. Remove from the heat and stir in the chocolate chips until melted. Add the vegan buttery spread and heat over low heat, stirring until smooth. (This chocolate sauce is not only delicious on peanut butter pie. Try spreading it on your lover . . . but wait until it cools).

Pour the chocolate sauce evenly over the peanut butter filling. Smooth the top with a rubber spatula and chill for at least 2 hours so the chocolate topping becomes firm.

Store loosely covered with plastic wrap in the refrigerator and use within 1 week.

Consider extending marriage rights to the other foods in your pantry. Why should peanut butter and chocolate be the only ones allowed to wed? Let's spread the love, broaden the spectrum of flavorful pairings, and brighten our plates with glittering diversity. Amen, sister friend!

Every third Thursday of the month, my girlfriends come on over, and we stay up half the night talking about our issues and eating vegan cheesecake. Truth be told, I do most of the talking, and they do most of the eating. Around four in

COCONUTTY GINGER *cheesecake*

CRUST

1½ cups **finely ground ginger-snap cookies** (store-bought)

¼ cup **raw cashews, finely ground**

¼ cup **coconut oil, liquefied**

¼ teaspoon **salt**

FILLING

2 tablespoons **Ener-G Egg Replacer**

½ cup **water**

3 cups **firm Coconutty Cream Cheese** (page 133; see Tricks of the Trade)

¾ cup **sugar**

2 teaspoons **freshly squeezed lemon juice**

1 teaspoon **vanilla extract**

TOPPING (OPTIONAL)

1 cup **Ruby-Red Syrup** (page 134)

Hey, girl, hey, let's start by making a gingery crust. Lightly coat a 9-inch springform pan with vegetable shortening. Sprinkle with flour and then shake and tap out the excess.

Put the gingersnaps, cashews, coconut oil, and salt in a medium bowl. Stir until well combined. Press the mixture into the bottom of the prepared pan. Chill for at least 1 hour so the crust can set.

Once the crust has set, you have my permission to put this cheesecake together. Listen to your Mistress—don't rush the process.

Preheat the oven to 350 degrees F.

Combine the egg replacer and water in a food processor and process until frothy, about 3 minutes. Add the Coconutty Cream Cheese, sugar, lemon juice, and vanilla extract. Process until creamy and well combined, about 3 minutes, stopping as needed to scrape down the work bowl with a rubber spatula.

Pour into the crust and smooth the top with a rubber spatula. Bake for 50 minutes, or until the top is somewhat firm and just beginning to brown.

Let cool in the springform pan for 10 minutes before removing the exterior ring. Let cool for at least 1 additional hour before slicing. Serve each slice with a generous drizzling of Ruby-Red Syrup, if desired.

Store loosely covered with plastic wrap in the refrigerator and use within 1 week.

Per serving: 330 calories, 8 g protein, 13 g fat (7 g sat), 46 g carbohydrates, 292 mg sodium, 62 mg calcium, 1 g fiber

TRICKS OF THE TRADE

- For finely ground cashews, put the cashews in a dry high-speed blender and process until finely ground. You may need to stop the processing

the morning when I stop talking, I discover that they've eaten all but one slice of the cheesecake, and that they left about three hours ago. Woe is me! Only one slice left!

once or twice to scrape down the container and dislodge any cashews that have become stuck around the blade.

- For finely ground gingersnap cookies, put the gingersnaps in a dry food processor and process until finely ground. As an alternative, put the gingersnaps in a sealed ziplock bag and roll over the bag with a rolling pin until the cookies are finely ground. The latter option will give you an outlet for those aggressions that have been bottled up since that lunchroom fiasco in the third grade. I can still hear them: "We're not laughing *at* you, Ginger. We're laughing *with* you." Dammit, I wasn't laughing!

- Hey, girlie girl, plan ahead. The Coconutty Cream Cheese used in this recipe must be prepared in advance and chilled for at least 3 hours so that it's firm enough to use when making this cheesecake.

In a flaming hurry?

You don't have to make your own Coconutty Cream Cheese for this recipe. Instead, use three 8-ounce containers of store-bought nondairy cream cheese. Let soften at room temperature before using to make your cheesecake filling. And, if you're in a real razzle-dazzle rush, you can also use a prepared vegan graham cracker crust rather than making your own. Of course, you couldn't call this a Coconutty *Ginger* Cheesecake then, since you'd be leaving out the ginger, and you'd just have to find another way to pay homage to me. A statue in your town square will suffice.

COCONUTTY CHOCOLATE CHEESECAKE: You may do without the ginger in your cheesecake, but the only way I could forgive you for that slap in the face is if you replace the ginger with chocolate (the only worthy substitute that can even begin to compare). Instead of using gingersnap cookies to make the crust, use crispy chocolate cookies that don't have cream fillings, unless you want an oily mess in your oven. Save the oily mess for your bedroom.

After much trial and error, and forty pounds of residual weight gain, I've perfected a vegan pound cake. Be warned—you'll have your lovers in the palm of your pretty hand once you feed this to them. They'll be in a dessert-induced euphoria, and they'll want to express their gratitude to you the best way they know how. Oh goody! I can think of no better way to burn off these calories.

pound-me CAKE

2 cups **all-purpose white flour**

2 teaspoons **baking powder**

½ teaspoon **salt**

½ cup **firm silken tofu**

1 cup **sugar**

½ cup **coconut oil**

2 teaspoons **vanilla extract**

½ teaspoon **hazelnut extract** (optional)

¾ cup **full-fat coconut milk**

Preheat the oven to 325 degrees F. Lightly coat a 9 x 5-inch loaf pan with vegetable shortening. Sprinkle with flour and then shake and tap out the excess. (Gently tap now and save the hardcore pounding for later.)

Put the flour, baking powder, and salt in a medium bowl. Stir using a dry whisk until well combined.

Blend the tofu in a food processor until creamy.

Using an electric mixer, combine the sugar and coconut oil in a large bowl. Add the vanilla extract, optional hazelnut extract, and tofu. Mix until well combined.

Beat in half the coconut milk. Then beat in about half the dry mixture. Repeat with the remaining coconut milk and dry mixture, adding both gradually to avoid lumps. Mix until just blended. The batter will be thick.

Scoop the batter into the prepared pan and smooth the top with a rubber spatula. Bake for 55 to 60 minutes, or until a toothpick inserted in the center comes out clean.

Let cool in the pan on a cooling rack for 30 minutes. Remove from the pan and let cool for at least 1 hour longer before slicing. Store tightly wrapped in plastic wrap in the refrigerator and use within 1 week.

Looking for someone to share your Pound-Me Cake with? Just know that at this very moment there are plenty of people pounding the pavement looking for a slice of Pound-Me Cake baked only the way you know how to make it. Get out there, pound the pavement yourself, and find 'em. Then let the pounding begin!

Per serving: 380 calories, 6 g protein, 19 g fat (16 g sat), 47 g carbohydrates, 256 mg sodium, 86 mg calcium, 1 g fiber

TRICKS OF THE TRADE: You may have noticed that Pound-Me Cake requires only ¾ cup of coconut milk, but most cans of coconut milk give you 1¾ cups of that creamy white stuff. What's a showgirl to do with the leftover milk? Bathe in it? Well, that's one option, but I have an even better idea, a perfectly delicious solution. Use it to make Crème Anglaise for Strawberry Shortcake (page 158). Bingo, I'm brilliant. Eat now; thank me later.

Here it is—the pièce de résistance! This cake is so damn decadent that it's downright uncivilized! It's certainly not health food, so don't try to convince yourself that it is. Give in, you brute. These unruly amounts of fat and sugar and refined flour are to be saved for a special occasion, like Tuesday.

barbarian TORTE

CAKE

1 cup **plain nondairy milk**

2 teaspoons **freshly squeezed lemon juice**

2 ounces **unsweetened chocolate**

2 tablespoons **Ener-G Egg Replacer**

¼ cup **warm water**

1¾ cups **unbleached all-purpose flour**

1½ cups **sugar**

1 teaspoon **salt**

1 teaspoon **baking soda**

½ teaspoon **baking powder**

⅓ cup **canola oil**

(continues on page 157)

Barbarians: You'll need to pretend to be civilized if you hope to pull off this torte. You got me? Good. Now proceed.

Preheat the oven to 350 degrees F. Cut a piece of parchment paper into two circles, both with a 9-inch diameter to fit the bottom of two 9-inch baking pans. Insert the parchment circles into the pans and lightly coat the sides with vegetable shortening. Sprinkle with flour and then shake and tap out the excess.

To make the cake, mix the nondairy milk with the lemon juice in a small bowl. Set aside.

Put the unsweetened chocolate in a small saucepan over very low heat, stirring constantly until melted. Remove from the heat.

Put the egg replacer and water in a food processor and process until frothy, about 3 minutes.

Sift the flour, sugar, salt, baking soda, and baking powder into a large bowl. Add the oil and half the nondairy milk mixture. Using an electric mixer, beat until just mixed, about 1 minute.

Add the remaining nondairy milk mixture and the melted chocolate and egg replacer mixture. Beat until just mixed, about 1 minute, to make a batter.

Working quickly, divide the batter between the prepared pans. Bake for 30 to 35 minutes, or until a toothpick inserted in the center comes out clean. (You dirty brute, do you even know the meaning of the word "clean"?)

Let cool in the pans on a cooling rack for 1 hour. Turn the cakes out of the pans onto the rack and let cool for 1 to 2 hours longer.

While the cakes cool, prepare the filling. Remove the coconut milk from the fridge, but do not shake the cans. (When chilled, the cream from the

CREAM FILLING

2 (15-ounce) cans **full-fat coconut milk, chilled for 6 to 8 hours**

8 ounces **nondairy cream cheese, softened**

⅔ cup **light brown sugar, packed**

1 teaspoon **vanilla extract**

⅛ teaspoon **salt**

CHOCOLATE DUST

1 (3.5-ounce) **nondairy dark chocolate bar, grated**

coconut milk rises to the top.) Gently turn the cans upside down and carefully remove the lids. Pour the watery liquid into a storage container and reserve for other purposes (see Tricks of the Trade, page 161). Scoop the coconut cream from the cans and put it in a large bowl. Using the electric mixer, beat the cream until fluffy, about 5 minutes.

Put the nondairy cream cheese, brown sugar, vanilla extract, and salt in a large bowl and blend until well combined using the electric mixer (there's no need to clean it after beating the coconut cream). Add the cream cheese mixture to the coconut cream and mix until well combined.

Once the cakes have cooled completely, cut each cake in half horizontally to make four layers. Be careful to cut the cakes evenly, you vulgar savage. (I hope you'll take that as a compliment. Some of my best lovers have been vulgar savages. Actually, *all* my lovers have been vulgar savages.)

To assemble the cake, put one layer on a cake plate, spread one-quarter of the filling over that layer, and sprinkle with 1 to 2 tablespoons of the chocolate dust. Continue to alternate the layers, the filling, and the chocolate dust until all four layers are stacked with a layer of the filling separating them. Spread the remaining filling over the top layer of the cake. Delicately sprinkle with the remaining chocolate dust as a garnish. Geez Louise, I said *delicately* sprinkle! This isn't one of your barnyard escapades.

Chill for at least 2 hours before serving to all your beastly friends. Store loosely covered with plastic wrap in the refrigerator and use within 1 week—as if you could restrain yourself for longer than that, you wild heathen, you.

Per serving: 350 calories, 4 g protein, 21 g fat (11 g sat), 40 g carbohydrates, 345 mg sodium, 156 mg calcium, 2 g fiber

Here again, we have a universally adored treat that's been veganized. This time, I pointed my vegan ray gun at the decadent strawberry shortcake of my youth, which basically consisted of a store-bought pound cake dressed with marinated strawberries and a luscious custard sauce. When the veganizing was all said and done, what I got was a recipe for jaw-dropping goodness in your mouth. Note that you'll have to make Pound-Me Cake (page 152) for this recipe to be complete, but don't we all want an excuse for anything called Pound-Me Cake to enter our lives? I know I do.

strawberry SHORTCAKE

CAKE

1 **Pound-Me Cake** (page 152)

CRÈME ANGLAISE

½ cup **raw cashews**

¾ cup **unsweetened nondairy milk**

1 cup **full-fat coconut milk**

½ cup **sugar**

1½ tablespoons **nutritional yeast**

1½ teaspoons **vanilla extract**

MARINATED STRAWBERRIES

3 cups **strawberries, hulled and halved**

¼ cup **sugar**

3 tablespoons **Kirsch** (optional; see Tricks of the Trade, page 56)

While the Pound-Me Cake is in the oven, whip up the Crème Anglaise, or custard sauce. Process the cashews in a blender on high speed until finely ground. Add the nondairy milk and blend for 1 minute. Add the coconut milk, sugar, nutritional yeast, and vanilla extract and blend until well combined, about 1 minute.

Transfer the mixture to a medium saucepan. Cook over medium-high heat while gently stirring with a wire whisk until the mixture begins to bubble, about 5 minutes. Decrease the heat to medium and cook, stirring constantly with the whisk, until the sauce thickens, about 5 minutes. Remove from the heat and let sit for 10 minutes to cool slightly. Transfer to a container, cover, and chill for at least 1 hour.

Combine the strawberries, sugar, and optional Kirsch in a medium bowl. Set aside to marinate at room temperature for at least 1 hour.

Assemble the shortcake just before serving. Prepare your guests for the dessert experience of a lifetime. Let them know that dessert will be served shortly and that they should turn off all cell phones and beepers and take a few deep breaths. For each serving, put one ¾-inch-thick slice of Pound-Me Cake on a small dessert plate or in a small bowl. Top with about ¼ cup of the strawberries, with juice. Drizzle about ¼ cup of the Crème Anglaise over the strawberries and cake. Serve immediately, savor entirely, and swoon completely.

Per serving: 562 calories, 8 g protein, 28 g fat (21 g sat), 73 g carbohydrates, 282 mg sodium, 141 mg calcium, 3 g fiber

Bundt. Bundt. I love the word "Bundt." There's something downright provocative about that word. I don't know what it is. And then there's "lemon poppy seeds." Something about the flavor of perky lemon combined with nutty poppy seeds just spins my windmills. Now put these things together, and I'm a happy camper, a very happy camper, a very campy happy camper. This classic lemon–poppy seed Bundt cake is perfect for a late afternoon tea party with all your girlfriends . . . and a few burly truckers.

LEMON-POPPY *bundt*

CAKE

2½ cups **unbleached all-purpose flour**

1 cup **sugar**

2 teaspoons **baking powder**

½ teaspoon **baking soda**

¼ teaspoon **salt**

½ cup **firm silken tofu**

¾ cup **plain nondairy milk**

½ cup **canola oil**

¼ cup **freshly squeezed lemon juice**

2 teaspoons **vanilla extract**

2 tablespoons **lemon zest**

2 teaspoons **poppy seeds**

LEMON ICING

1¼ cups **powdered sugar**

2 tablespoons **freshly squeezed lemon juice**

½ teaspoon **poppy seeds,** for garnish

Bundt fans, listen up! Preheat the oven to 350 degrees F. Lightly coat a 9- or 10-inch Bundt pan with vegetable shortening. Sprinkle with flour and then shake and tap out the excess.

Put the flour, sugar, baking powder, baking soda, and salt in a large bowl. Stir with a dry whisk until well combined.

Put the tofu in a food processor and process until completely smooth. Add the nondairy milk, oil, lemon juice, and vanilla extract. Process until well combined.

Pour the wet mixture into the dry mixture and stir until just combined. The batter will be thick. Fold in the lemon zest and the 2 teaspoons of poppy seeds. Don't forget those poppy seeds!

Scoop the batter into the prepared pan and smooth the top using a rubber spatula.

Bake for 40 minutes, or until a toothpick inserted in the cake comes out clean. Let cool in the pan for 10 minutes, and then turn the cake out onto a cooling rack. Let the cake cool for at least 2 hours before icing.

When the cake has cooled, prepare the icing. Sift the powdered sugar into a large bowl. Add the 2 tablespoons of lemon juice and stir until the juice has absorbed all the sugar and an icing forms.

Put the cake on a plate or cake platter. Drizzle the icing along the top ridge of the cake, allowing the icing to naturally drip down the sides. Try to cover most of the cake with the icing in this way. Lightly sprinkle the ½ teaspoon of poppy seeds over the cake. Chill for at least 1 hour before serving.

Campy happy campers: Store leftover cake in a tightly sealed container in the refrigerator and use within 1 week.

Per serving: 223 calories, 3 g protein, 8 g fat (1 g sat), 36 g carbohydrates, 129 mg sodium, 131 mg calcium, 1 g fiber

Homemade dairy-free ice cream can be yours with the flip of a switch! No ice-cream maker or other contraption required. You need only a food processor, a few commonly found ingredients, and a high threshold for total chocolate immersion. This cool treat is deceptively wholesome. It masquerades as pure decadence but is really composed of some very respectable whole foods. Since "Guilt-free Indulgence" is my middle name, this dessert is right up my alley. Care to join me? Indulge, my sweet, indulge!

ICED *cocoa cream*

1 cup **mashed ripe bananas** (about 2 bananas)

1 cup **mashed ripe avocados** (about 2 avocados)

¼ cup **unsweetened cocoa powder**

3 tablespoons **agave nectar**

½ teaspoon **vanilla extract**

Put all the ingredients in a food processor. Process until the mixture is well combined. If you feel so inclined, mimic the whirling blade of the food processor with a gyrating motion of your voluptuous rear. This will help you to work up an appetite for some Iced Cocoa Cream—and to be the best showgirl you can be.

Pour the mixture into a storage container and cover with a tightly sealed lid. Freeze for at least 3 hours until completely frozen. Before serving, let sit at room temperature for about 10 minutes to thaw slightly.

Iced Cocoa Cream will keep in the freezer for up to 2 weeks . . . unless you devour it before then. Chances are, it will be gone within a few days, or my name isn't Mistress "Guilt-free Indulgence" Ginger.

Per serving: 215 calories, 2 g protein, 10 g fat (2 g sat), 28 g carbohydrates, 36 mg sodium, 3 mg calcium, 4 g fiber

COCOA-MINT DREAM: Add ½ teaspoon of peppermint extract before processing the Iced Cocoa Cream.

COCOA-PEANUT RIPPLE: After processing the Iced Cocoa Cream, add ¼ cup of salted smooth peanut butter, 1 teaspoon at a time, and pulse until mixed but not fully blended.

COCOA-RASPBERRY SWIRL: After processing the Iced Cocoa Cream, add ⅔ cup of fresh raspberries and pulse until mostly blended, leaving some small bits of berries.

This decadent dessert topping is made mostly from coconut cream, one of those miracles of vegan cookery. It can be whipped into a heavenly fluff much like dairy whipping cream (minus the incarcerated cows). Once you add a little sugar and vanilla extract, you've got the perfect topping for a fruit crisp, a pumpkin pie, or my left butt cheek.

Tenderly whipped TOPPING

1 (15-ounce) can **full-fat coconut milk, chilled for 6 to 8 hours**

3 tablespoons **powdered sugar**

2 teaspoons **vanilla extract**

Pinch **ground nutmeg**

When ready to use, remove the coconut milk from the fridge, but do not shake the can. (When chilled, the cream from the coconut milk rises to the top.) Gently turn the can upside down and carefully remove the lid. Pour the watery liquid into a storage container and reserve for other purposes (see Tricks of the Trade). Scoop the coconut cream from the can and put it in a large bowl.

Using an electric mixer, beat the coconut cream on high until fluffy, about 5 minutes.

Add the powdered sugar, vanilla extract, and nutmeg and mix until just incorporated. Refrigerate until ready to serve. Store leftovers in a tightly sealed container in the refrigerator and use within 5 days. Do not, I repeat, do not, try to store your Tenderly Whipped Topping in the nightstand by your bed. Although it will be conveniently close-at-hand, it will not stay fresh. I had to learn this the hard way.

Per ¼ cup: 140 calories, 1 g protein, 12 g fat (10 g sat), 8 g carbohydrates, 17 mg sodium, 0 mg calcium, 0 g fiber

TRICKS OF THE TRADE: Hold it right there! Don't pour that watery liquid from the coconut milk down the drain. Instead, use it to replace a portion of the water in the Green Gulp (page 24), and have yourself an electrolyte-packed purifying smoothie. "Waste not, want not," so they say. I don't know if I totally agree. I'm never wasteful, but I'm always wanting, or so my lovers tell me.

The Continuing Adventures of You

Darling peeps, have I piqued your interest on the subject of veganism? Would you like to know more about all that the vegan lifestyle encompasses and how to make it work for you? Wonderful! I'm thrilled to know that I've got your compassionate juices flowing. Now let's keep those juices flowing with some of my favorite films, books, websites, and periodicals. These resources will help you to further explore veganism, going deeper into the subjects of factory farming, moral philosophy, nutritional know-how, and cruelty-free living. Your Mistress commands that the continuing adventures of you commence forthwith!

WAKE UP

whatcamebefore.com

This eleven-minute video offers a concise look at how animals are raised for food on modern farms. The disturbing images of standard practices on factory farms are juxtaposed with images of healthy, happy animals on farm sanctuaries. Alternatives to a meat-based diet are suggested so that you are empowered with ideas about how you can help.

Earthlings

This 2005 documentary is a comprehensive account of how animals are used for food, clothing, entertainment, and scientific research. The video footage of violence toward animals is graphic, and you only need to see it once to understand how animals are affected by our everyday choices.

EAT OUT

vegguide.org

VegGuide.org is a community-maintained, worldwide guide to vegetarian and vegan restaurants and shopping. I find the website to be very practical, especially when I have a last-minute dinner date. I just hop on VegGuide to see what local restaurants offer delectable vegan options and get the night of debauchery started off right.

GET SOME GOOD VEGAN GOODS

In need of some vegan shoes, belts, purses, cosmetics, or specialty foods? While some of these cruelty-free items may be found in your hometown, mail-order options abound. Here are a few of the leading distributors that I recommend:

alternativeoutfitters.com

Alternative Outfitters is an online vegan boutique specializing in non-leather shoes, handbags, belts, apparel, and accessories. Doll yourself up the cruelty-free way every day.

veganstore.com

Pangea is a cruelty-free source where you can find, among other things, shoes, bags, belts, cosmetics, and body-care items. I especially appreciate the selection of gift baskets that I can send to a friend whenever I'm feeling the need to spread the love. (And those same gift baskets can be sent my way, in case you were wondering. Ahem.)

veganessentials.com

Vegan Essentials also offers a variety of vegan products, including specialty foods that you're not likely to find in your local natural food store. Vegan Danish Kringle, anyone? Yes, please.

KNOW YOUR NUTRITION

Becoming Vegan: Express Edition
by Brenda Davis, RD, and Vesanto Melina, MS, RD

Learn how to fuel your dancing machine the vegan way. That's what I did! Soon after going vegan years ago, I read the first edition of this book, and look at me now. I'm friggin' gorgeous, not to mention happy and healthy.

veganhealth.org

This user-friendly website is devoted to vegan nutrition and offers current and reliable information on everything from basic meal planning to sports nutrition to food allergies.

GET INSPIRED

Animal Liberation by Peter Singer

If you, like me, operate not only from your heart but also your head, I recommend that you pick up a copy of this classic text. Get the nitty-gritty on the reason behind the vegan. Peter Singer deftly elucidates the ethics that can prompt anyone to go vegan. It's one of the first things that I read when my curiosity about vegetarianism was piqued, and you can see where that led: Veganville, USA!

Eating Animals by Jonathan Safran Foer

This engrossing read is another wake-up call for meat eaters. Before his child was born, Jonathan Safran Foer decided to take an honest look at the foods he was consuming. He investigated the sources of his meat-based diet and saw firsthand how "food animals" are raised and slaughtered. This book relays his experiences in eye-opening stories that are likely to ignite your own inner awakenings.

The World Peace Diet by Will Tuttle, PhD

This book shines a light on the spiritual ramifications of eating animals and unabashedly advocates a vegan lifestyle as the ultimate pathway to healing for our world. Taking a universal approach to spirituality, Will Tuttle illuminates the bigger picture, revealing how the exploitation of animals is inextricably tied to the oppression and suffering of all and how we can alleviate these cycles of suffering through everyday choices that reflect an open heart's convictions.

Grass Roots Veganism with Jo Stepaniak, vegsource.com/jo/

If you want to nurture your inner Glinda, this comprehensive website is a great place to start. Jo Stepaniak's site provides information on all aspects of vegan living. Jo was my go-to sage when I first went vegan; each time I frequent the site I find some new gem of wisdom. On the site, Jo moderates a discussion board where a community of like-minded people discuss the joys and challenges of vegan living. The "Ask Jo! Archives" will likely answer your burning questions on the subject of veganism, including everything from basic philosophy to more practical concerns, and Jo writes brilliantly on the subject of compassion. Her essays invite us to uncover our own compassion and widen its reach to inform how we treat animals, other humans, ourselves, and our planet.

Food for Thought Podcast
with Colleen Patrick-Goudreau, compassionatecook.com

Not one for reading? Not a problem. Just turn to Colleen Patrick-Goudreau's podcast for a dose of inspiration that you can absorb any ol' time your brain isn't otherwise occupied, like when you're cleaning the house or polishing your rhinestones. Each of these informative episodes features a fresh commentary on a wide range of vegan-related subjects. With a mission to debunk the myths surrounding veganism, Colleen has a no-nonsense, accessible approach that'll get you revved up for some joyful vegan living.

STAY IN THE SWING OF THINGS

VegNews, vegnews.com

Get the scoop on what's hot and the dish on the delish. You'll find yourself feeling a part of the global vegan community and further inspired to have your vegan heyday today and every day. This award-winning print magazine is published six times a year and always offers a colorful collection of tantalizing articles and recipes, and the website is equally fabulous, upbeat, and trendy.

SPREAD THE WORD

For some people, the desire to help animals will lead them to do more than eschew animal products. If you find that you'd like to get more active on behalf of animals, you may connect with any number of local or national organizations that advocate for animals. These organizations are also excellent places to connect with communities of like-minded individuals. To learn more about one approach to vegan activism that can be done anywhere, visit Vegan Outreach at veganoutreach.org.

Acknowledgments

As much I like sequins and sass, and as much as Mistress Ginger wants to sing and dance her way into the hearts of all, my primary reason for writing this book was to be a voice for those who cannot speak for themselves. I wrote this book for creatures who can fly, swim, crawl, or walk but have spent their lives in confinement, unable to move according to their individual impulses and their natural instincts.

When So-hi, my beloved Siamese cat of eleven years, passed away in 2001, I was prompted to take a closer look at my own relationship with animals, to see how we are connected, and then to make changes in my life to reflect my new realizations. I am grateful to So-hi for leading me on this journey toward living in accordance with my respect for animals.

I also wrote this book for anyone who has suffered from a disease or condition that has been caused or exacerbated by the standard American diet and the consumption of animal products. I believe that a whole-foods plant-based diet is a pathway to healing, not only for our physical bodies but also for our hearts and minds, awakening us to our compassionate nature and allowing us to live in harmony with the world around us.

I acknowledge those members of the queer community—lesbian, gay, bisexual, and transgender—who continue on their own journeys toward liberation. I hope that we can recognize how all movements for liberation have striking parallels, how no one is free when others are oppressed, and how our daily choices can support freedom for everyone on all fronts.

I am grateful to the activists from all these movements; they have taught me about the importance of these issues, have worked diligently and passionately for liberation, and are building loving communities for those who identify with these efforts for change. I have been especially inspired by Compassionate Action for Animals, a nonprofit that operates with absolute integrity as its members advocate for farmed animals. I am thankful for the opportunities that I've had to support their mission, to be a part of their team, and to learn from their sterling example of respectful, nonviolent activism.

I am grateful to the staff at Book Publishing Company for allowing me to share this book with the world, for helping to shape my vision for this book, and for being instrumental in bringing that vision to life. Thanks especially to Bob and Cynthia Holzapfel for taking a bold chance on Ginger and to Ellen Foreman for being a dynamic support throughout the process. To my dear friend Jo Stepaniak, who has been the editor of my dreams and the inspiration of a lifetime, thank you. Through your editorial encouragement, this book became more than I dreamed it could be, and through your own writings on veganism and compassionate living, I have been continually and profoundly moved.

I'd like to acknowledge the team that made Ginger look so damn good. Thanks to Michael Frear at the Chair Salon for shaping up Ginger's coif and to Stephen Herzog at the Do Hair Salon for helping Ginger to once and for all decide on a signature look. To photographer Erik Saulitis, thanks for embracing this project with gusto and for producing such glorious photos of Ginger in the kitchen. And speaking of the kitchen, thanks to David Fey and Michael Putman for sharing theirs and permitting Ginger and her swarthy crew to spend a day prancing around in that stunning space. Big hunky thanks to Ginger's entourage of stud-muffin models: José Victor Bueno, Joey Clark, Joe Crook, Jim Domenick, Brentt Flammang, Patrick Jeffrey, George Maurer, and Zack Teska. You took my breath away with the generous offerings of your time, your enthusiasm, your beauty, and your brawn.

Thanks to my dear friends, the "Dinner at 8" crew, who have happily tested my recipes and frolicked with me and Ginger over the years: Sarah Barrett, Jodi Davidson Bennett, Joey Clark, Valerie Kann Gibson, Rachel Hiltsley, Rachel Holder Hennig, Jeffry Lusiak, Stephen Magner, Dustin Maxwell, Chrissy Baker Rishavy, Glen Straight, Emily Tyra, Freeman Wicklund, and Beth Disharoon Wright. Thanks to Anna Alger Tolladay for serving me stuffed artichokes in Pebble Beach, to Alton "Buddy" Porter for making that giant burrito bowl for me, to Caroline Fermin for teaching me how to make Brazilian beans, and to Andi Scott Dumas for inspiring me to transport everyone to Morocco with some broccoli salad. I send a special shout-out to E.G. Nelson, my queer-ass vegan baking comrade; Jim Domenick, my ever-ready panda-bear-in-waiting; and Brooke Murphy, my vivacious partner in crime who helped me to unearth Ginger from wherever she was lying dormant. To Andra and Ernesta Corvino, who fed me pesto when I was but a fledgling showgirl, thank you. You showed me how wonderful it can be to share a meal with friends, and how friends can become family.

And speaking of family, thanks to my beloved family, Paula and Frank Leaf, Tasha Brown, and Jessica Cooley, for years of love and support. To Mom, the greatest cook I have ever known, thanks for passing along your favorite recipes for me to veganize, as well as your sense of humor and sense of style. Mistress Ginger has made use of all those things!

To my precious Siamese children, Lewis and Pearl, thank you for helping to sustain my energy and motivation for writing of this book. Feeling your unconditional affection, I was renewed, and seeing the spirit shining through your eyes, I was inspired.

I am grateful for the Siddha Yoga path and my teacher Gurumayi Chidvilsananda for being an abiding presence in my life and imparting a deepening experience of love, light, and peace.

Thanks to my many lovers. (Ginger is not the only one who gets some action now and then!) I too have learned a lot from my lovers, from the vegan ones who took me on magical adventures, made vegan nachos for me, and gave me a sense of community to the non-vegan ones who gifted me with waffle irons, brought me food from their gardens, and ate my "vegan schmeegan" food gladly.

And finally, to Mistress Ginger, that ever-present showgirl, thanks for showing up in my life just when I needed you and reminding me how to shine, how to play, how to sing, how to be free. You inspire me, and I hope that our book will serve to inspire others in the same way.

JUSTIN LEAF

About the Author

Justin Leaf is a performance artist, dance teacher, and yoga teacher living in Minneapolis. Since graduating from the Juilliard School in 2001 with a bachelor of fine arts in dance performance, Justin has been a ballet dancer by day with James Sewell Ballet and Minnesota Dance Theatre. By night, Justin has infiltrated the Twin Cities cabaret circuit with performances that bring together his dancerly chops, his passion for vocal performance, and the creature that is Mistress Ginger. Vegan since 2002, Justin has advocated for animal rights as an active member of Compassionate Action for Animals. To learn more about Justin and all his endeavors, visit justinleaf.com.

Photo by Amy Jeanchaiyaphum

INDEX

BookPublishing Co.

books that educate, inspire, and empower

To find your favorite vegetarian and soyfood products online, visit:
healthy-eating.com

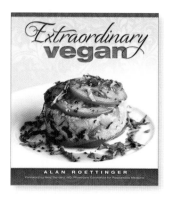

Extraordinary Vegan

Alan Roettinger

978-1-57067-296-5 • $19.95

Grills Gone Vegan

Tamasin Noyes

978-1-57067-290-3 • $19.95

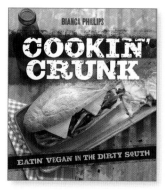

Cookin' Crunk

Bianca Phillips

978-1-57067-268-2 • $19.95

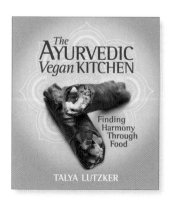

The Ayurvedic Vegan Kitchen

Talya Lutzker

978-1-57067-286-6 • $19.95

Soak Your Nuts:
Karyn's Conscious Comfort Foods

Karyn Calabrese

978-1-57067-275-0 • $19.95

Artisan Vegan Cheese

Miyoko Schinner

978-1-57067-283-5 • $19.95

Purchase these health titles and cookbooks from your local bookstore or natural food store,
or you can buy them directly from:

Book Publishing Company • P.O. Box 99 • Summertown, TN 38483 • 800-695-2241

Please include $3.95 per book for shipping and handling.